COMMUNICATION GAMES & ACTIVITY MASTERS

WORD BY WORD

Second Edition

Steven J. Molinsky • Bill Bliss

Contributing Author
Melinda Roberts

Illustrated by
Richard E. Hill

Word by Word Communication Games

Pearson Education, 10 Bank Street, White Plains, NY 10606

Editorial director: Pam Fishman
Vice president, director of design and production: Rhea Banker
Director of electronic production: Aliza Greenblatt
Director of manufacturing: Patrice Fraccio
Senior manufacturing manager: Edith Pullman
Marketing director: Oliva Fernandez
Production editor: Diane Cipollone
Assistant editor: Katherine Keyes
Senior digital layout specialist: Lisa Ghiozzi
Text design: Lisa Ghiozzi
Cover design: Warren Fischbach
Illustrations: Richard E. Hill

ISBN 978-0-13-191625-8; 0-13-191625-4

Pearson Longman on the Web
PearsonLongman.com offers online resources for teachers and students. Access our Companion Websites, our online catalog, and our local offices around the world.

Visit us at **pearsonlongman.com**.

Printed in the United States of America
1 2 3 4 5 6 7 8 9 10—V012—19 18 17 16 15 14 13 12 11 10

Introduction

Word by Word Communication Games & Activity Masters is intended to serve as a resource for dynamic, interactive activities to accompany the second edition of the *Word by Word Picture Dictionary*. These 113 multi-level activities, along with their accompanying reproducible Activity Masters, have been designed to reinforce the vocabulary presented in each unit of the *Word by Word Picture Dictionary* through pair, group, and full-class interaction.

Overview of Activity Types

The following types of activities are included:

Board Games—*group* activities in which students play a game that reviews vocabulary through a variety of questions and tasks

Classroom Search Games—*full-class* activities in which students circulate around the classroom and ask their classmates questions

Concentration Games—*group* activities for vocabulary reinforcement in which students attempt to remember the location of visuals and their corresponding word cards

Drawing Games—*team* activities in which students compete to finish a drawing

Group Competition—*group* activities in which students compete to answer questions

Group Discussion—*group* activities in which students discuss problem situations and then report back to the class

Information Gaps—*pair* activities in which students ask and answer questions in order to gain missing information

Interviews—*pair* activities in which students interview each other and then report back to the class about what they learned

Listening Games—*pair* activities in which students listen for information and then react or respond accordingly

Listening Grids—*full-class* activities in which students arrange visuals on a grid and then listen for clues that match the arrangement they have chosen

Matching Games—*group* and *full-class* activities in which students circulate around the classroom giving clues to each other in an attempt to find their appropriate "matches"

Memory Games—*group* activities in which students respond based on information they remember

Pair Competition—*pair* activities in which students compete to accomplish tasks

Pick-a-Card Games—*pair* activities in which students look for matches for cards they are holding

Picture Differences—*pair* activities in which students work together to identify differences in two pictures

Team Competition—*team* activities in which students compete to answer questions and complete tasks

Tell-a-Story—*group* activities in which students write a story based on a set of visuals

Word Clue Games—*pair* activities in which pairs compete to guess items based on clues

Game Book Overview

The following are provided for each of the Communication Games:

- The activity type

- The corresponding *Word by Word Picture Dictionary* pages

- The grouping arrangement—pairs, groups, teams, full-class

- The corresponding reproducible Activity Masters found at the back of the book

- A brief description of the activity

- A *Getting Ready* section with instructions for before-class preparation of materials needed for the activity

- Step-by-step instructions for doing the activity in class

The Game Book activities are designated as *one-star, two-star,* and *three-star* based on their level of difficulty.

- *One-star* activities are simple, structured activities in which students typically identify and match visuals or ask and answer simple questions.

- *Two-star* activities typically require students to listen for information to identify vocabulary words, answer multiple questions, perform tasks, or remember and reconstruct information. Challenging *two-star* activities, in which students must perform several tasks or remember a significant amount of information, are designed as *two-star/ three-star* activities.

- *Three-star* activities are typically highly unstructured, with much room for student input and interpretation.

Be sure to review the vocabulary in the corresponding *Word by Word Picture Dictionary* lessons before doing each activity.

There are several strategies for pairing students for pair activities. You might want to pair students by ability, since students of similar ability might work more efficiently together than students of dissimilar ability. On the other hand, you might wish to pair a weaker student with a stronger one. The slower student benefits from this pairing, while the more advanced student strengthens his or her abilities by helping a partner.

We encourage you to modify or adapt these activities in any way you feel would be appropriate for your students. In keeping with the spirit of *Word by Word*, they are intended to provide students with a vocabulary-learning experience that is dynamic . . . interactive . . . and fun!

Steven J. Molinsky
Bill Bliss

CONTENTS

Appendix

Activity Masters

Game Index

MISSING INFORMATION *
INFORMATION GAP
Picture Dictionary Page 1

ACTIVITY MASTERS
1 & 2

THE ACTIVITY

Students ask and answer questions in order to find out missing information.

GETTING READY

Students will do this activity in pairs. Make copies of Activity Master 1 (*Registration Form A*) for half the class and Activity Master 2 (*Registration Form B*) for the other half of the class.

● **1.** Divide the class into pairs.

● **2.** Give a copy of *Registration Form A* to one member of each pair and a copy of *Registration Form B* to the other.

● **3.** Write the following questions on the board and have the class practice saying them:

> What's your first name?
> What's your middle initial?
> What's your last name?
> What's your address?
> What's your apartment number?
> What's your zip code?
> What's your telephone number?
> What's your cell phone number?
> What's your e-mail address?
> What's your social security number?
> What's your sex?
> What's your place of birth?

● **4.** Tell the class that each member of the pair has different information. The object of the activity is for each member of the pair to fill in their missing information by asking questions. For example:

> A. What's your first name?
> B. Tracy.
> A. How do you spell "Tracy"?
> B. T-R-A-C-Y.

● **5.** When the pairs have completed filling in their forms, have them read their answers to each other to make sure they have written the information correctly.

1.2

THE SOUZA FAMILY *
INFORMATION GAP
Picture Dictionary Pages 2–3

ACTIVITY MASTERS
3 & 4

THE ACTIVITY

Students work together to complete a family tree.

GETTING READY

Students will do this activity in pairs. Make copies of Activity Master 3 (*The Souza Family A*) for half the class and Activity Master 4 (*The Souza Family B*) for the other half of the class.

- **1.** Divide the class into pairs.

- **2.** Give a copy of *The Souza Family A* to one member of each pair and a copy of *The Souza Family B* to the other.

- **3.** Tell students that each member of the pair knows the names of different people in the Souza family. Have them ask each other questions to find out the missing names and then write them under the appropriate people. (Have students ask for the spelling of names if they aren't sure.) For example:

  A. Who is Jane's husband?
  B. Richard.
  A. How do you spell "Richard"?
  B. R-I-C-H-A-R-D.

- **4.** When they have completed the activity, have students compare their family trees.

1.3

FAMILY & PERSONAL INFORMATION
BOARD GAME **

BOARD GAME

Picture Dictionary Pages 1–3

THE ACTIVITY

Students play a board game that focuses on personal information and family members.

GETTING READY

Students will do this activity in groups. Make a copy of Activity Master 5 (*Family & Personal Information Board Game*) and Activity Master 6 (*Family Member Cards*) for each group. Cut each copy of Activity Master 6 into separate cards.

Each group will need a die. You can duplicate Activity Master 7 (*Game Cube*) to make a die for each group, or students can use a coin. Each player will also need a marker (a button or anything small) and a piece of paper.

- **1.** Divide the class into small groups.

- **2.** Give a copy of the *Family & Personal Information Board Game* and a set of *Family Member Cards* to each group. Also provide each group with a die, markers, and a piece of paper. If students use a coin as a die, the class should decide which side of the coin will indicate a move of one space and which will indicate a move of two spaces.

- **3.** Have students place their markers on *Start*. The group should decide who goes first. That student begins the game by rolling the cube (or flipping the coin) and moving his or her marker. If the student responds to the question or task correctly, he or she may take one more turn. (The group decides if the response is correct.) If the student doesn't respond correctly, the next student takes a turn. No one may take more than two turns at a time.

  Option 1: The first person to reach *Finish* is the winner.

  Option 2: The game continues until each student reaches *Finish*. This way everybody is a winner.

UNIT 2

MY CLASSROOM **
LISTENING GAME
Picture Dictionary Pages 4–5, 8

PAIRS

ACTIVITY MASTERS
8 & 9

THE ACTIVITY

Students ask and answer questions in order to find out about the location of items in a classroom.

GETTING READY

Students will do this activity in pairs. Make a copy of Activity Master 8 (*My Classroom*) and Activity Master 9 (*Classroom Object Cards*) for each student. Cut each copy of Activity Master 9 into separate cards.

● **1.** Divide the class into pairs.

● **2.** Give each student a copy of *My Classroom* and a set of *Classroom Object Cards*.

● **3.** Write the following questions and answers on the board and have students practice saying them:

> A. Is there a screen in your classroom?
> B. Yes, there is. It's to the left of the chalkboard.
>
> A. Is there a calculator in your classroom?
> B. Yes, there is. It's on the student's desk, next to the ruler.
>
> A. Is there an overhead projector in your classroom?
> B. No, there isn't.

● **4.** Have each Student A choose eight classroom object cards and place them anywhere they wish in the classroom.

● **5.** Student B asks Yes/No questions about the objects in Student A's classroom and arranges his or her cards so that they match what Student A has described. Then, have students compare to make sure their classroom objects are in the same locations.

● **6.** When students have finished the activity, have them reverse roles and play again.

CLASSROOM & CLASSROOM ACTIONS
BOARD GAME **/***
BOARD GAME
Picture Dictionary Pages 4–8

ACTIVITY MASTERS
7, 10, & 11

THE ACTIVITY

Students play a board game that focuses on the classroom and classroom actions.

GETTING READY

Students will do this activity in groups. Make a copy of Activity Master 10 (*Classroom & Classroom Actions Board Game*) and Activity Master 11 (*Classroom Action Cards*) for each group. Cut each copy of Activity Master 11 into separate cards.

Each group will need a die. You can duplicate Activity Master 7 (*Game Cube*) to make a die for each group, or students can use a coin. Each player will also need a marker (a button or anything small) and a piece of paper.

● **1.** Divide the class into small groups.

● **2.** Give a copy of the *Classroom & Classroom Actions Board Game* and a set of *Classroom Action Cards* to each group. Also provide each group with a die, markers, and a piece of paper. If students use a coin as a die, the class should decide which side of the coin will indicate a move of one space and which will indicate a move of two spaces.

● **3.** Have students place their markers on *Start*. The group should decide who goes first. That student begins the game by rolling the cube (or flipping the coin) and moving his or her marker. If the student responds to the question or task correctly, he or she may take one more turn. (The group decides if the response is correct.) If the student doesn't respond correctly, the next student takes a turn. No one may take more than two turns at a time.

Option 1: The first person to reach *Finish* is the winner.

Option 2: The game continues until each student reaches *Finish*. This way everybody is a winner.

WHAT DO YOU DO EVERY DAY? *
CLASSROOM SEARCH
Picture Dictionary Pages 9–11

ACTIVITY MASTER
12

THE ACTIVITY

Students walk around the classroom asking each other about the things they do every day.

GETTING READY

Students will do this activity as a class. Make a copy of Activity Master 12 (*What Do You Do Every Day?*) for each student in the class.

● **1.** Give a copy of *What Do You Do Every Day?* to each student.

● **2.** Write the following on the board for students to use as a framework for asking each other questions:

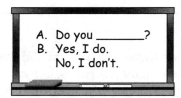

> A. Do you _____?
> B. Yes, I do.
>   No, I don't.

● **3.** Have students walk around asking each other the question on the board. When students have found someone who does one of the activities on their grids, the responding student should write his or her name in that square of the grid (only one signature is necessary for each square).

The student whose grid is filled with the most signatures is the winner of the game.

TWO FAMILIES AT HOME TODAY *
PICTURE DIFFERENCES
Picture Dictionary Pages 9–11

THE ACTIVITY

Students work together to find differences between the activities of two families.

GETTING READY

Students will do this activity in pairs. Make copies of Activity Master 13 (*The Lopez Family at Home*) for half the class and Activity Master 14 (*The Gomez Family at Home*) for the other half of the class.

- **1.** Divide the class into pairs.

- **2.** Give a copy of *The Lopez Family at Home* to one member of each pair and a copy of *The Gomez Family at Home* to the other.

- **3.** Tell students that the object of the game is to find eight differences between the two pictures. Do one example before beginning the game. For example:

   In the Lopez family, the father is cleaning the house.
   In the Gomez family, the father is doing the laundry.

- **4.** When the activity is completed, call on students to tell the differences they found between the two scenes.

ANSWER KEY

The Lopez Family	The Gomez Family
The father is cleaning the house.	The father is doing the laundry.
The mother is washing the dishes.	The mother is making lunch.
The older son is feeding the cat.	The older son is reading the newspaper.
The younger son is watching TV.	The younger son is playing the guitar.
The older daughter is ironing.	The older daughter is exercising.
The younger daughter is listening to music.	The younger daughter is reading a book.
The grandmother is using the computer.	The grandmother is writing a letter.
The grandfather is playing cards.	The grandfather is listening to the radio.

2.5

DAILY ROUTINES *
INFORMATION GAP
Picture Dictionary Pages 9–11

PAIRS

ACTIVITY MASTERS
15 & 16

THE ACTIVITY

Students work together to learn about two people's daily routines.

GETTING READY

Students will do this activity in pairs. Make copies of Activity Master 15 (*Alan's Daily Routine*) for half the class and Activity Master 16 (*Ellen's Daily Routine*) for the other half of the class.

● **1.** Divide the class into pairs.

● **2.** Give a copy of *Alan's Daily Routine* to one member of each pair and a copy of *Ellen's Daily Routine* to the other.

● **3.** Write the following on the board for students to use as a framework for asking and answering questions:

> A. What does (Alan/Ellen) do before work?
> B. He/She _____.
> A. Then what does he/she do?
> B. He/She _____.
> A. What does he/she do after that?
> B. He/She _____.
>   Etc.

● **4.** Tell the class that one person has a list of the things Alan usually does before and after work every day and the other person has a description of Ellen's daily routine. The object of the activity is for the person with Alan's information to find out about Ellen and the person with Ellen's information to find out about Alan.

● **5.** When the pairs have completed the activity, have them compare their schedules.

EVERYDAY ACTIVITY BOARD GAME **
BOARD GAME
Picture Dictionary Pages 9–11

**ACTIVITY MASTERS
7, 17, & 18**

THE ACTIVITY

Students play a board game that focuses on everyday and leisure activities.

GETTING READY

Students will do this activity in groups. Make a copy of Activity Master 17 (*Everyday Activity Board Game*) and Activity Master 18 (*Everyday Activity Pantomime Cards*) for each group. Cut each copy of Activity Master 18 into separate cards.

Each group will need a die. You can duplicate Activity Master 7 (*Game Cube*) to make a die for each group, or students can use a coin. Each player will also need a marker (a button or anything small).

● **1.** Divide the class into small groups.

● **2.** Give a copy of the *Everyday Activity Board Game* and a set of *Everyday Activity Pantomime Cards* to each group. Also provide each group with a die and markers. If students use a coin as a die, the class should decide which side of the coin will indicate a move of one space and which will indicate a move of two spaces.

● **3.** Have students place their markers on *Start*. The group should decide who goes first. That student begins the game by rolling the cube (or flipping the coin) and moving his or her marker. If the student responds to the question or task correctly, he or she may take one more turn. (The group decides if the response is correct.) If the student doesn't respond correctly, the next student takes a turn. No one may take more than two turns at a time.

Option 1: The first person to reach *Finish* is the winner.

Option 2: The game continues until each student reaches *Finish*. This way everybody is a winner.

2.7 WHAT'S NEW? NOT MUCH. *
PICK-A-CARD
Picture Dictionary Pages 12–13

THE ACTIVITY

Pairs of students attempt to get rid of all their cards by finding appropriate responses for conversation cards in their hands.

GETTING READY

Students will do this activity in pairs. Make two copies of Activity Master 19 (*Everyday Conversation Cards*) for each pair. Cut each copy of Activity Master 19 into separate cards.

● **1.** Divide the class into pairs.

● **2.** Give each pair two sets of *Everyday Conversation Cards*.

● **3.** Have students shuffle the cards, take six cards each, and leave the remaining cards in a pile. The pair should then decide which player will go first.

● **4.** Each player looks at his or her cards and puts any matching conversation pairs in a pile face up. Player 1 must now attempt to find the match for the cards remaining in his or her hand. To do so, the player says one of the "A" lines. For example: "What's new?" If Player 2 has the appropriate "B" line, he or she responds: "Not much" and gives the card to Player 1, who puts the matching cards in his or her pile. If Player 2 doesn't have the card, he or she tells Player 1: "Sorry! Keep looking!" In that case, Player 1 must *keep looking* by picking a card from the pile. It is now Player 2's turn to ask for a card.

The game continues until one player has no cards in his or her hand. The player with the most matching pairs wins the game.

2.8

EVERYDAY CONVERSATION
BOARD GAME **/***
BOARD GAME
Picture Dictionary Pages 12–13

ACTIVITY MASTERS
7 & 20

THE ACTIVITY

Students play a board game that focuses on everyday conversational exchanges.

GETTING READY

Students will do this activity in groups. Make a copy of Activity Master 20 (*Everyday Conversation Board Game*) for each group.

Each group will need a die. You can duplicate Activity Master 7 (*Game Cube*) to make a die for each group, or students can use a coin. Each player will also need a marker (a button or anything small).

● **1.** Divide the class into small groups.

● **2.** Give a copy of the *Everyday Conversation Board Game* to each group. Also provide each group with a die and markers. If students use a coin as a die, the class should decide which side of the coin will indicate a move of one space and which will indicate a move of two spaces.

● **3.** Have students place their markers on *Start*. The group should decide who goes first. That student begins the game by rolling the cube (or flipping the coin) and moving his or her marker. If the student responds to the question or task correctly, he or she may take one more turn. (The group decides if the response is correct.) If the student doesn't respond correctly, the next student takes a turn. No one may take more than two turns at a time.

Option 1: The first person to reach *Finish* is the winner.

Option 2: The game continues until each student reaches *Finish*. This way everybody is a winner.

WORLD-WIDE WEATHER TODAY *
INFORMATION GAP
Picture Dictionary Page 14

THE ACTIVITY

Students work together to find out information about weather and temperatures in different cities around the world.

GETTING READY

Students will do this activity in pairs. Make copies of Activity Master 21 (*World-Wide Weather A*) for half the class and Activity Master 22 (*World-Wide Weather B*) for the other half of the class.

● **1.** Divide the class into pairs.

● **2.** Give a copy of *World-Wide Weather A* to one member of each pair and a copy of *World-Wide Weather B* to the other.

● **3.** Tell students that each member of the pair knows the weather and temperatures in different cities around the world. Have them ask each other questions to find out the missing information and then write the information in their charts. For example:

    A. How's the weather in _____?
    B. It's _____. / [There are thunderstorms.]
    A. What's the temperature?
    B. It's _____ degrees Fahrenheit.

● **4.** When the pairs have completed the activity, have them compare their charts.

3.1

TIME, MONEY, & DATE SEARCH *
CLASSROOM SEARCH
Picture Dictionary Pages 15–19

CLASS

**ACTIVITY MASTER
23**

THE ACTIVITY

Students walk around the classroom asking each other about time, money, and calendar dates.

GETTING READY

Students will do this activity as a class. Make a copy of Activity Master 23 (*Time, Money, & Date Search*) for each student in the class.

- **1.** Give a copy of *Time, Money, & Date Search* to each student.

- **2.** Write the following on the board for student reference during the activity:

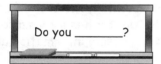

Do you _____?

- **3.** Have students walk around asking each other the questions on the Activity Master. When students have found someone who answers "yes" to one of the questions on their grids, the responding student should write his or her name in that square of the grid (only one signature is necessary for each square).

   The student whose grid is filled with the most signatures is the winner of the game.

IMPORTANT DATES FOR THE WONG FAMILY **

INFORMATION GAP

Picture Dictionary Pages 15–19

PAIRS

ACTIVITY MASTERS
24 & 25

THE ACTIVITY

Students work together to find out important dates for the Wong family this year.

GETTING READY

Students will do this activity in pairs. Make copies of Activity Master 24 (*Wong Family Calendar A*) for half the class and Activity Master 25 (*Wong Family Calendar B*) for the other half of the class.

● **1.** Divide the class into pairs.

● **2.** Give a copy of *Wong Family Calendar A* to one member of each pair and a copy of *Wong Family Calendar B* to the other.

● **3.** Tell students that something important is happening every month in the Wong family. Student A has information about half of the events and Student B has information about the others. The goal of the activity is to find out the missing information and write it below each month on the calendar.

● **4.** Write the following on the board for students to use as a reference as they do the activity:

> What's happening on January 19th?
> What's happening on February 3rd?
>   etc.

● **5.** When the pairs have completed the activity, have them compare their calendars.

3.3 NUMBER-TIME-MONEY-CALENDAR
GAME * or **
TEAM COMPETITION
Picture Dictionary Pages 15–19

THE ACTIVITY

Teams compete to answer questions about numbers, time, money, and the calendar.

GETTING READY

Note: You can do this as four separate *one-star* games, using just the *Number, Time, Money,* or *Calendar* cards, or you can do this as a combined *two-star* game, using as many cards from each category as you wish.

Students will do this activity in teams. Make a copy of Activity Master 26 (*Number Questions*), Activity Master 27 (*Time Questions*), Activity Master 28 (*Money Questions*), and Activity Master 29 (*Calendar Questions*). Cut the Activity Masters into separate cards. You will also need a watch with a second hand or a timer for this activity.

- **1.** Divide the class into two teams.
- **2.** Place the cards in a pile face down on a table or desk in front of the room. (If you do this as a combined activity, you can place the cards from each category together, or mix the category cards.)
- **3.** Students from each team take turns picking a card from the pile. They must attempt to answer it in 10 seconds. If an answer is correct, their team earns a point. If not, a member of the other team has a chance to respond to that team's question before choosing his or her own card. If neither team answers successfully, the card goes to the bottom of the pile.

  The team with the most points is the winner of the game.

4.1 WHAT'S DIFFERENT ABOUT THESE LIVING ROOMS? *
PICTURE DIFFERENCES
Picture Dictionary Page 21

**ACTIVITY MASTERS
30 & 31**

THE ACTIVITY

Students work together to find differences between two living rooms.

GETTING READY

Students will do this activity in pairs. Make copies of Activity Master 30 (*Bruno's Living Room*) for half the class and Activity Master 31 (*Brenda's Living Room*) for the other half of the class.

● **1.** Divide the class into pairs.

● **2.** Give a copy of *Bruno's Living Room* to one member of each pair and a copy of *Brenda's Living Room* to the other.

● **3.** Ask students what living room items they see in the pictures. Together, brainstorm a list of vocabulary and write the words on the board.

● **4.** Tell students that the object of the game is to find ten differences between the two living rooms. Do one example before beginning the game. For example:

> In Bruno's living room, there's one floor lamp.
> In Brenda's living room, there are two floor lamps.

● **5.** When the activity is completed, call on students to tell the differences they found between the two living rooms.

ANSWER KEY

In Bruno's Living Room	In Brenda's Living Room
There's one floor lamp.	There are two floor lamps.
There's an end table next to the loveseat.	There's an end table next to the sofa.
There's a plant on the coffee table.	There's a plant on the end table.
There's one picture over the fireplace.	There are two pictures over the fireplace.
There are two throw pillows on the sofa.	There's one throw pillow on the sofa.
There's a rug under the coffee table.	There isn't a rug in the living room.
There's one speaker in the wall unit.	There are two speakers in the wall unit.
There's a DVD player on top of the TV.	There isn't a DVD player.
There's a magazine holder next to the armchair.	There's a magazine holder next to the loveseat.
There's a fireplace screen in front of the fireplace.	There isn't a fireplace screen.

WHAT'S THE HOUSEHOLD ITEM? **
LISTENING GRID
Picture Dictionary Pages 21–26

THE ACTIVITY

Students place pictures on a grid and then turn them over based on sentences they hear.

GETTING READY

Students will do this activity as a class. Make a copy of Activity Master 32 (*Listening Grid*) and Activity Master 33 (*Household Item Cards*) for each student. Cut each copy of Activity Master 33 into separate cards.

---

1. Give each student a *Listening Grid* and a set of *Household Item Cards*.

2. Tell students to choose nine of the cards and place them on the grid, face up, in any order they wish.

3. Say the following sentences in random order and tell students to turn over any card that you have described:

> You put this in front of a fireplace.
> You put these on your windows.
> This holds magazines.
> You put this next to a sofa.
> You serve food in this.
> You put flowers in this.
> You eat with this.
> You keep dishes in this in the dining room.
> You put your head on this when you sleep.
> This tells the time and helps you get up in the morning.
> You keep your clothes in this.
> You put this on the bed when you sleep.
> You put this in your hand when you hold something hot.
> This is a book with recipes.
> You use this to wash the dishes.
> This keeps food cold.
> The baby sleeps here.
> The baby plays with this.
> The baby sits in this.
> The baby goes for a ride in this.
> You brush your teeth with this.
> You use this after you take a shower.
> You use this to dry your hair.
> You use this to clean the bathtub.

4. The first person to have three turned-over cards in a straight line—either vertically, horizontally, or diagonally—wins the game. Have the winner call out the sentences to check accuracy.

4.3

AT HOME BOARD GAME **
BOARD GAME
Picture Dictionary Pages 21–27

ACTIVITY MASTERS
7, 34, & 35

THE ACTIVITY

Students play a board game that focuses on items in the home.

GETTING READY

Students will do this activity in groups. Make a copy of Activity Master 34 (*At Home Board Game*) and Activity Master 35 (*Home Object Cards*) for each group. Cut each copy of Activity Master 35 into separate cards.

Each group will need a die. You can duplicate Activity Master 7 (*Game Cube*) to make a die for each group, or students can use a coin. Each player will also need a marker (a button or anything small) and a piece of paper.

- **1.** Divide the class into small groups.

- **2.** Give a copy of the *At Home Board Game* and a set of *Home Object Cards* to each group. Also provide each group with a die, markers, and a piece of paper. If students use a coin as a die, the class should decide which side of the coin will indicate a move of one space and which will indicate a move of two spaces.

- **3.** Have students place their markers on *Start*. The group should decide who goes first. That student begins the game by rolling the cube (or flipping the coin) and moving his or her marker. If the student responds to the question or task correctly, he or she may take one more turn. (The group decides if the response is correct.) If the student doesn't respond correctly, the next student takes a turn. No one may take more than two turns at a time.

   Option 1: The first person to reach *Finish* is the winner.

   Option 2: The game continues until each student reaches *Finish*. This way everybody is a winner.

4.4  THE BUILDING ON MAPLE STREET *
INFORMATION GAP
Picture Dictionary Pages 28–29

PAIRS

ACTIVITY MASTERS
36 & 37

THE ACTIVITY

A student who is looking for an apartment asks another student, the realtor, for some information.

GETTING READY

Students will do this activity in pairs. Make copies of Activity Master 36 (*Tell Me About the Building*) for half the class and Activity Master 37 (*Information About the Building*) for the other half of the class.

- **1.** Divide the class into pairs.

- **2.** Give a copy of *Tell Me About the Building* to one member of each pair (Student A) and a copy of *Information About the Building* to the other (Student B).

- **3.** Explain that Student A is looking for an apartment to rent. Student B is a realtor and has information about a very nice apartment on Maple Street.

- **4.** Student A asks questions about the building and the apartment and fills in the answers based on Student B's responses.

- **5.** When the pairs have completed the activity, tell Student A to check the realtor's information to make sure he or she has written the correct answers to the questions.

 4.5

WHAT'S DIFFERENT ABOUT THESE HOUSES? *
PICTURE DIFFERENCES
Picture Dictionary Pages 30–31

PAIRS

ACTIVITY MASTERS
38 & 39

THE ACTIVITY

Students work together to find differences between the household problems in two houses.

GETTING READY

Students will do this activity in pairs. Make copies of Activity Master 38 (*The Wilsons' House*) for half the class and Activity Master 39 (*The Watsons' House*) for the other half of the class.

- **1.** Divide the class into pairs.

- **2.** Give a copy of *The Wilsons' House* to one member of each pair and a copy of *The Watsons' House* to the other.

- **3.** Tell students that the object of the game is to find eight differences between the problems these households are having. Do one example before beginning the game. For example:

      In the Wilsons' house, the bathtub is leaking.
      In the Watsons' house, the sink is leaking.

- **4.** When the activity is completed, call on students to tell the differences they found between the two houses.

ANSWER KEY

In the Wilsons' House	In the Watsons' House
The bathtub is leaking.	The sink is leaking.
The hot water heater isn't working.	The toilet is broken.
The roof is leaking.	The paint is peeling.
The stove isn't working.	The refrigerator is broken.
There are ants in the kitchen.	There are mice in the kitchen.
The lock is broken.	The TV isn't working.
The chimney is dirty.	The steps are broken.
The tiles are loose in the bathroom.	The doorbell doesn't ring.

NAME THAT HOUSEHOLD ITEM! **/***
WORD CLUE GAME
Picture Dictionary Pages 32–35

THE ACTIVITY

Pairs of students will compete against other pairs of students to guess household items from clues given by their partners.

GETTING READY

Students will do this activity in pairs, competing against another pair of students. Make two copies of Activity Master 40 (*Household Item Word Clue Cards*) for each group of four students. Cut each copy of the Activity Master into separate cards.

1. Divide the class into groups of four. Then divide each group into two teams—Team A and Team B.

2. Give each team a set of *Household Item Word Clue Cards*.

3. Have the teams shuffle the cards and place them face down in a stack.

4. Tell students that the object of the game is to listen to clues from their partners to guess the household item on the card. Students will sit across from their partners. The partner will give up to three clues. Each clue is worth one point. If the student isn't able to name the item, the card goes to the bottom of the pile and the pair is given three points.

   The game continues until all the cards have been guessed. The team with the *least number of points* wins the game.

  DOWNTOWN RIVERDALE *
INFORMATION GAP
Picture Dictionary Pages 36–39

ACTIVITY MASTERS
41 & 42

5.1

THE ACTIVITY

Students work together to identify all the buildings in the town of Riverdale.

GETTING READY

Students will do this activity in pairs. Make copies of Activity Master 41 (*Downtown Riverdale A*) for half the class and Activity Master 42 (*Downtown Riverdale B*) for the other half of the class.

- **1.** Divide the class into pairs.

- **2.** Give a copy of *Downtown Riverdale A* to one member of each pair and a copy of *Downtown Riverdale B* to the other.

- **3.** Tell students that they know some of the buildings in Riverdale and their partners know the other buildings. The object of the activity is for each of them to find out the names of all the buildings and write them on their maps.

- **4.** Start the activity by telling students to look at the gas station at the bottom of their maps. Ask: "What's across from the gas station?" Have the students holding Map B tell you: "The shoe store." Tell all the students with Map A to write *shoe store* in that building on their handout.

- **5.** Continue the activity by having the members of each pair ask each other about the buildings that aren't identified on their maps. When students find out the name of a building, they should write it on their maps.

- **6.** When the pairs have filled in their maps, have them check their partner's map to make sure they wrote the correct names in the correct buildings.

5.2

WHAT'S IN YOUR NEIGHBORHOOD? *
PICK-A-CARD
Picture Dictionary Pages 36–39

PAIRS

ACTIVITY MASTER
43

THE ACTIVITY

Pairs of students attempt to get rid of all their cards by finding matches for cards in their hands.

GETTING READY

Students will do this activity in pairs. Make two copies of Activity Master 43 (*Places in My Neighborhood Cards*) for each pair. Cut each copy of Activity Master 43 into separate cards.

- **1.** Divide the class into pairs.

- **2.** Give each pair two sets of *Places in My Neighborhood Cards*.

- **3.** Write the following questions and answers on the board and have students practice saying them:

  > A. Is there a (*bakery*) in your neighborhood?
  > B. Yes, there is.
  >
  > A. Is there a (*book store*) in your neighborhood?
  > B. Sorry, there isn't. Keep looking!

- **4.** Have students shuffle the cards, take six cards each, and leave the remaining cards in a pile. The pair should then decide which player will go first.

- **5.** Each player looks at his or her cards and puts any matching pairs in a pile face up. Player A must now attempt to find the match for the cards remaining in his or her hand. To do so, the player asks: "Is there a _____ in your neighborhood?" If Player B has that card, he or she responds: "Yes, there is" and gives the card to Player A, who puts the matching cards in his or her pile. If Player B doesn't have the card, he or she tells Player A: "Sorry, there isn't. Keep looking!" In that case, Player A must *keep looking* by picking a card from the pile. It is now Player B's turn to ask for a card.

  The game continues until one player has no cards in his or her hand. The player with the most matching pairs wins the game.

WHAT'S THE PLACE? **
LISTENING GRID
Picture Dictionary Pages 36–39

ACTIVITY MASTERS
32 & 44

THE ACTIVITY

Students place pictures on a grid and then turn them over based on sentences they hear.

GETTING READY

Students will do this activity as a class. Make a copy of Activity Master 32 (*Listening Grid*) and Activity Master 44 (*Places Around Town Cards*) for each student. Cut each copy of Activity Master 44 into separate cards.

1. Give each student a *Listening Grid* and a set of *Places Around Town Cards.*

2. Tell students to choose nine of the cards and place them on the grid, face up, in any order they wish.

3. Say the following sentences in random order and tell students to turn over any card that you have described:

> This is a place where people buy bread and rolls.
> This is a place where people buy books.
> This is a place where people buy cars.
> This is a place where people go to see a doctor.
> This is a place where people buy clothing.
> This is a place where people buy computers.
> This is a place where people buy donuts.
> This is a place where people buy flowers.
> This is a place where people buy furniture.
> This is a place where people get gas.
> This is a place where people buy food.
> This is a place where people exercise.
> This is a place where people buy ice cream.
> This is a place where people wash their clothes.
> This is a place where people see movies.
> This is a place where people can buy cats and dogs.
> This is a place where people mail letters and packages.
> This is a place where students study.
> This is a place where people buy shoes.
> This is a place where people buy toys.

4. The first person to have three turned-over cards in a straight line—either vertically, horizontally, or diagonally—wins the game. Have the winner call out the sentences to check accuracy.

5.4 BUILD A CITY! **
LISTENING GAME
Picture Dictionary Pages 36–41

PAIRS

ACTIVITY MASTERS
45 & 46

THE ACTIVITY

One student instructs another where to put buildings on a city map.

GETTING READY

Students will do this activity in pairs. Make copies of Activity Master 45 (*Build a City!*) and Activity Master 46 (*Build-a-City Cards*) for each student. Cut each copy of Activity Master 46 into separate cards.

● **1.** Divide the class into pairs.

● **2.** Give each student a copy of *Build a City!* and a set of *Build-a-City Cards.*

● **3.** Tell all the Student As in each pair to *build a city* by placing the build-a-city cards any place they wish on the map.

● **4.** Student A then directs Student B to build the same city by instructing Student B where to place the cards on his or her map, using prepositions such as:

next to	to the right/left of
across from	on _____ (Street/Avenue)
in front of	at the intersection of _____ and _____
on the right/left	on the corner of _____ and _____

● **5.** Student B must follow Student A's directions without looking at Student A's map.

● **6.** When Student B's map is complete, have the partners compare their maps to see if they match.

● **7.** Then have students switch roles. Student B *builds a city* and gives instructions to Student A.

5.5

NAME THAT PLACE! **/***
WORD CLUE GAME
Picture Dictionary Pages 36–41

THE ACTIVITY

Pairs of students will compete against other pairs of students to guess places in the community from clues given by their partners.

GETTING READY

Students will do this activity in pairs, competing against another pair of students. Make two copies of Activity Master 47 (*Places Around Town Word Clue Cards*) for each group of four students. Cut each copy of the Activity Master into separate cards.

- **1.** Divide the class into groups of four. Then divide each group into two teams—Team A and Team B.

- **2.** Give each team a set of *Places Around Town Word Clue Cards.*

- **3.** Have the teams shuffle the cards and place them face down in a stack.

- **4.** Tell students that the object of the game is to listen to clues from their partners to guess the place on the card. Students will sit across from their partners. The partner will give up to three clues. Each clue is worth one point. If the student isn't able to name the item, the card goes to the bottom of the pile and the pair is given three points.

    The game continues until all the cards have been guessed. The team with the *least number of points* wins the game.

PLACES AROUND TOWN BOARD GAME **
BOARD GAME
Picture Dictionary Pages 36–41

ACTIVITY MASTERS
7, 48, & 49

THE ACTIVITY

Students play a board game that focuses on places around town.

GETTING READY

Students will do this activity in groups. Make a copy of Activity Master 48 (*Places Around Town Board Game*) and Activity Master 49 (*Guess-the-Place Cards*) for each group. Cut each copy of Activity Master 49 into separate cards.

Each group will need a die. You can duplicate Activity Master 7 (*Game Cube*) to make a die for each group, or students can use a coin. Each player will also need a marker (a button or anything small) and a piece of paper.

● **1.** Divide the class into small groups.

● **2.** Give a copy of the *Places Around Town Board Game* and a set of *Guess-the-Place Cards* to each group. Also provide each group with a die, markers, and a piece of paper. If students use a coin as a die, the class should decide which side of the coin will indicate a move of one space and which will indicate a move of two spaces.

● **3.** Have students place their markers on *Start*. The group should decide who goes first. That student begins the game by rolling the cube (or flipping the coin) and moving his or her marker. If the student responds to the question or task correctly, he or she may take one more turn. (The group decides if the response is correct.) If the student doesn't respond correctly, the next student takes a turn. No one may take more than two turns at a time.

Option 1: The first person to reach *Finish* is the winner.

Option 2: The game continues until each student reaches *Finish*. This way everybody is a winner.

6.1

DO YOU REMEMBER WHAT THEY LOOK LIKE? **

MEMORY GAME

Picture Dictionary Page 42–45

PAIRS

**ACTIVITY MASTERS
50 & 51**

THE ACTIVITY

Students look at pictures of two different families and try to remember the differences between them.

GETTING READY

Students will do this activity in pairs. Make copies of Activity Master 50 (*The Markov Family & The Pavlov Family*) and Activity Master 51 (*Do You Remember What They Look Like?*) for each pair.

● **1.** Divide the class into pairs.

● **2.** Give each pair a copy of *The Markov Family & The Pavlov Family.*

● **3.** Tell students that they will have 3 minutes to study the pictures carefully and try to remember the differences between these people—for example, Mrs. Pavlov is short; Mrs. Pavlov is tall; Mr. Markov has a beard; Mr. Pavlov has a mustache. After they have studied the information, tell them to put the Activity Master aside.

● **4.** Next give each pair a copy of *Do You Remember What They Look Like?* Have them work together to answer the questions based on their memory of the pictures on Activity Master 50.

● **5.** When students have completed answering the questions, have them look at Activity Master 50 again to check their answers.

ANSWER KEY

1. short / tall
2. beard / mustache
3. heavy / thin
4. blond / black
5. straight / curly
6. long / shoulder-length
7. heavy / average weight
8. fancy / plain
9. large / small

DESCRIPTION & EMOTION BOARD GAME **
BOARD GAME
Picture Dictionary Pages 42–47

THE ACTIVITY

Students play a board game that focuses on descriptions and emotions.

GETTING READY

Students will do this activity in groups. Make a copy of Activity Master 52 (*Description & Emotion Board Game*).

Each group will need a die. You can duplicate Activity Master 7 (*Game Cube*) to make a die for each group, or students can use a coin. Each player will also need a marker (a button or anything small).

---

1. Divide the class into small groups.

2. Give a copy of the *Description & Emotion Board Game* to each group. Also provide each group with a die and markers. If students use a coin as a die, the class should decide which side of the coin will indicate a move of one space and which will indicate a move of two spaces.

3. Have students place their markers on *Start*. The group should decide who goes first. That student begins the game by rolling the cube (or flipping the coin) and moving his or her marker. If the student responds to the question or task correctly, he or she may take one more turn. (The group decides if the response is correct.) If the student doesn't respond correctly, the next student takes a turn. No one may take more than two turns at a time.

Option 1: The first person to reach *Finish* is the winner.

Option 2: The game continues until each student reaches *Finish*. This way everybody is a winner.

6.3

DESCRIPTION & EMOTION GUESSING
GAME * OR **
TEAM COMPETITION
Picture Dictionary Pages 42–47

THE ACTIVITY

Teams compete to answer questions about physical descriptions and emotions.

GETTING READY

Note: You can do this as three separate *one-star* games, using just the *Opposite, Pantomime,* or *Drawing* cards, or you can do this as a combined *two-star* game, using as many cards from each category as you wish.

Students will do this activity in teams. Make a copy of Activity Master 53 (*Opposite Adjective Cards*), Activity Master 54 (*Emotion Pantomime Cards*), and Activity Master 55 (*Description Drawing Cards*). Cut the Activity Masters into separate cards. You will also need a watch with a second hand or a timer for this activity.

● **1.** Divide the class into two teams.

● **2.** Place the cards in a pile face down on a table or desk in front of the room. (If you do this as a combined activity, you can place the cards from each category together, or mix the category cards.)

● **3.** Students from each team take turns picking a card from the pile. The student must come up with the opposite adjective in 10 seconds. The team must guess the emotion that the student pantomimes in 15 seconds. And the student must successfully draw the adjective pairs in 20 seconds. If an answer is correct, the team earns a point. If not, a member of the other team has a chance to respond to that team's question before choosing his or her own card. If neither team answers successfully, the card goes to the bottom of the pile.

The team with the most points is the winner of the game.

UNIT 7

A BIG SALE AT MENDOZA'S MARKET *
INFORMATION GAP
Picture Dictionary Page 48–49

PAIRS

ACTIVITY MASTERS
56 & 57

THE ACTIVITY

Students look at a supermarket flyer and ask and answer questions about prices for different food items.

GETTING READY

Students will do this activity in pairs. Make copies of Activity Master 56 (*Mendoza's Market A*) for half the class and Activity Master 57 (*Mendoza's Market B*) for the other half of the class.

- **1.** Divide the class into pairs.

- **2.** Give a copy of *Mendoza's Market A* to one member of each pair and a copy of *Mendoza's Market B* to the other.

- **3.** Tell students that each member of the pair knows the prices of different items on sale at Mendoza's Market. Have them ask each other questions to find out what the price is for items on their flyers and then write the price under the item. For example:

    A. How much are oranges?
    B. They're $3.75.

    A. How much are watermelons?
    B. They're $3.50.

- **4.** When the pairs have completed the activity, have them compare their supermarket flyers.

7.2

NAME THAT FRUIT!/NAME THAT VEGETABLE! **/***
WORD CLUE GAME
Picture Dictionary Pages 48–49

PAIRS

ACTIVITY MASTER
58

THE ACTIVITY

Pairs of students will compete against other pairs of students to guess fruits and vegetables from clues given by their partners.

GETTING READY

Students will do this activity in pairs, competing against another pair of students. Make two copies of Activity Master 58 (*Fruit & Vegetable Word Clue Cards*) for each group of four students. Cut each copy of the Activity Master into separate cards.

1. Divide the class into groups of four. Then divide each group into two teams—Team A and Team B.

2. Give each team a set of *Fruit & Vegetable Word Clue Cards*.

3. Have the teams shuffle the cards and place them face down in a stack.

4. Tell students that the object of the game is to listen to clues from their partners to guess the fruit or vegetable on the card. Students will sit across from their partners. The partner will give up to three clues. Each clue is worth one point. If the student isn't able to name the item, the card goes to the bottom of the pile and the pair is given three points.

   The game continues until all the cards have been guessed. The team with the *least number of points* wins the game.

7.3

LET'S GO SHOPPING! *
PICK-A-CARD
Picture Dictionary Pages 50–56

PAIRS

ACTIVITY MASTER
59

THE ACTIVITY

Pairs of students attempt to get rid of all their cards by finding matches for cards in their hands.

GETTING READY

Students will do this activity in pairs. Make two copies of Activity Master 59 (*Supermarket Shopping Cards*) for each pair. Cut each copy of Activity Master 59 into separate cards.

1. Divide the class into pairs.

2. Give each pair two sets of *Supermarket Shopping Cards*.

3. Write the following questions and answers on the board and have students practice saying them:

> A. Did you buy (*baby food*) at the supermarket?
> B. Yes, I did.
>
> A. Did you buy (*bread*) at the supermarket?
> B. Sorry. I didn't. Keep shopping!

4. Have students shuffle the cards, take six cards each, and leave the remaining cards in a pile. The pair should then decide which player will go first.

5. Each player looks at his or her cards and puts any matching pairs in a pile face up. Player A must now attempt to find the match for the cards remaining in his or her hand. To do so, the player asks: "Did you buy _____ at the supermarket?" If Player B has that card, he or she responds: "Yes, I did" and gives the card to Player A, who puts the matching cards in his or her pile. If Player B doesn't have the card, he or she tells Player A: "Sorry. I didn't. Keep shopping!" In that case, Player A must *keep shopping* by picking a card from the pile. It is now Player B's turn to ask for a card.

The game continues until one player has no cards in his or her hand. The player with the most matching pairs wins the game.

WHAT'S DIFFERENT ABOUT THESE SHOPPING TRIPS? *
PICTURE DIFFERENCES
Picture Dictionary Pages 50–56

7.4

ACTIVITY MASTERS
60 & 61

THE ACTIVITY

Students work together to find differences between two shopping trips to the supermarket.

GETTING READY

Students will do this activity in pairs. Make copies of Activity Master 60 (*Shirley's Trip to the Supermarket*) for half the class and Activity Master 61 (*Charlie's Trip to the Supermarket*) for the other half of the class.

- **1.** Divide the class into pairs.

- **2.** Give a copy of *Shirley's Trip to the Supermarket* to one member of each pair and a copy of *Charlie's Trip to the Supermarket* to the other.

- **3.** Tell students that the object of the game is to find eight differences between what these two people bought at the supermarket today. Do one example before beginning the game. For example:

  Shirley bought a pound of chicken.
  Charlie bought a pound of ground beef.

- **4.** When the activity is completed, call on students to tell the differences they found between what these people bought at the supermarket.

ANSWER KEY

Shirley bought . . .	Charlie bought . . .
a pound of chicken	a pound of ground beef
a bottle of salad dressing	a bottle of ketchup
a can of tuna fish	a can of coffee
a box of crackers	a box of cookies
a jar of pickles	a jar of olives
a bag of sugar	a bag of flour
a bunch of carrots	a bunch of grapes
a six-pack of water	a six-pack of soda

THE ACTIVITY

Teams compete to answer questions about foods.

GETTING READY

Students will do this activity in teams. Make a copy of Activity Master 62 (*Food & Supermarket Questions 1*) and Activity Master 63 (*Food & Supermarket Questions 2*). Cut the Activity Masters into separate cards. You will also need a watch with a second hand or a timer for this activity.

---

1. Divide the class into two teams.

2. Place *Food & Supermarket Questions 1* in a pile face down for Team 1 to use and *Food & Supermarket Questions 2* in a pile face down for Team 2 to use. Also, have paper and markers next to each team's set of cards.

3. Students from each team take turns picking a card from their team's pile. They must attempt to answer it in 15 seconds. If the answer is correct, their team earns a point. If not, a member of the other team has a chance to respond to that team's question before choosing his or her own card. If neither team answers successfully, the card goes to the bottom of the pile

   The team with the most points is the winner of the game.

7.6

COOKING QUESTION GAME **/*
TEAM COMPETITION**
Picture Dictionary Pages 57–59

**ACTIVITY MASTERS
64, 65, & 66**

THE ACTIVITY

Teams compete to respond to three different types of tasks, each progressing in difficulty.

GETTING READY

Students will do this activity in teams. Make a copy of Activity Master 64 (*Food Preparation Cards*), Activity Master 65 (*Kitchen Utensil Drawing Cards*), and Activity Master 66 (*Unit of Measure Question Cards*). Cut the Activity Masters into separate cards. You will also need a watch with a second hand or a timer for this activity.

● **1.** Divide the class into two teams.

● **2.** Place the three sets of cards on a desk or table in front of the room.

● **3.** A student from Team 1 comes to the front of the room and picks a *Food Preparation Card*. The student's task is to provide an object for the food preparation verb on the card. If the student answers correctly within 10 seconds, the team gets one point and the student can pick a *Kitchen Utensil Drawing Card*. The student draws the object on the board, and that team has 10 seconds to guess the object. If the team guesses correctly, the student then picks a *Unit of Measure Question Card*. The student reads the question and can consult with team members on the answer. If the team is able to answer the question correctly within 15 seconds, the team earns two points. Then a student from Team 2 comes to the front of the room to take his or her turn. If a student isn't able to answer correctly, a member of the other team has a chance to respond to that team's question before choosing his or her own card. If neither team answers successfully, the card goes to the bottom of the pile.

The team with the most points is the winner of the game.

RESTAURANT BOARD GAME **
BOARD GAME
Picture Dictionary Pages 60–64

ACTIVITY MASTERS
7 & 67

THE ACTIVITY

Students play a board game that focuses on fast food, the coffee shop, and the restaurant.

GETTING READY

Students will do this activity in groups. Make a copy of Activity Master 67 (*Restaurant Board Game*) for each group.

Each group will need a die. You can duplicate Activity Master 7 (*Game Cube*) to make a die for each group, or students can use a coin. Each player will also need a marker (a button or anything small).

---

1. Divide the class into small groups.

2. Give a copy of the *Restaurant Board Game* to each group. Also provide each group with a die and markers. If students use a coin as a die, the class should decide which side of the coin will indicate a move of one space and which will indicate a move of two spaces.

3. Have students place their markers on *Start*. The group should decide who goes first. That student begins the game by rolling the cube (or flipping the coin) and moving his or her marker. If the student responds to the question or task correctly, he or she may take one more turn. (The group decides if the response is correct.) If the student doesn't respond correctly, the next student takes a turn. No one may take more than two turns at a time.

Option 1: The first person to reach *Finish* is the winner.

Option 2: The game continues until each student reaches *Finish*. This way everybody is a winner.

UNIT 8

  WHAT DID YOU BUY AT THE MALL? *
MATCHING GAME
Picture Dictionary Page 65–70

ACTIVITY MASTER
68

THE ACTIVITY

Students tell what they bought at the mall in an attempt to find their match.

GETTING READY

Students will do this activity in groups. There are 20 cards in this activity. Divide your class into groups and use as many cards for each group as you wish.

Make two copies of Activity Master 68 (*Shopping Mall Match Cards*) for each group. Cut each copy of the Activity Master into separate cards.

● **1.** Divide your class into groups and give each student a different *Shopping Mall Match Card.*

● **2.** Write the following conversation on the board and have students practice it:

> A. What did you buy at the mall?
> B. I bought _____ and _____.

● **3.** Two items are depicted on each card. Based on their cards and using the conversation model on the board, have students walk around the room telling what they bought until they find their match.

● **4.** When all the students have found their matching partners, have them hold up their cards and tell what they bought. For example:

> Each of us bought a suit and a tie.
> Each of us bought pajamas and a bathrobe.

WHAT CLOTHING DO YOU HAVE? *
CLASSROOM SEARCH
Picture Dictionary Pages 65–70

THE ACTIVITY

Students walk around the classroom asking each other about clothing items they have.

GETTING READY

Students will do this activity as a class. Make a copy of Activity Master 69 (*What Clothing Do You Have?*) for each student in the class.

● **1.** Give a copy of *What Clothing Do You Have?* to each student.

● **2.** Write the following on the board for students to use as a framework for asking each other questions:

A. Do you have _____?
B. Yes, I do.
   No, I don't.

● **3.** Have students walk around asking each other the question on the board. When students have found someone who has one of the items on their grids, the responding student should write his or her name in that square of the grid (only one signature is necessary for each square).

The student whose grid is filled with the most signatures is the winner of the game.

WHAT'S ON SALE THIS WEEK? *
INFORMATION GAP
Picture Dictionary Pages 65–70

PAIRS

**ACTIVITY MASTERS
70 & 71**

THE ACTIVITY

Students look at a store flyer and answer questions about prices for different clothing and jewelry items.

GETTING READY

Students will do this activity in pairs. Make copies of Activity Master 70 (*Kovak's Department Store A*) for half the class and Activity Master 71 (*Kovak's Department Store B*) for the other half of the class.

- **1.** Divide the class into pairs.

- **2.** Give a copy of *Kovak's Department Store A* to one member of each pair and a copy of *Kovak's Department Store B* to the other.

- **3.** Tell students that each member of the pair knows the prices of different items on sale at Kovak's Department Store. Have them ask each other questions to find out what the price is for items on their flyers and then write the price under the item. For example:

    A. How much are skirts?
    B. They're $39.00.

    A. How much are blouses?
    B. They're $27.50.

- **4.** When the pairs have completed the activity, have them compare their store flyers.

CLOTHING BOARD GAME I ******
BOARD GAME
Picture Dictionary Pages 65–70

THE ACTIVITY

Students play a board game that focuses on clothing, footwear, jewelry, and accessories.

GETTING READY

Students will do this activity in groups. Make a copy of Activity Master 72 (*Clothing Board Game I*) for each group.

Each group will need a die. You can duplicate Activity Master 7 (*Game Cube*) to make a die for each group, or students can use a coin. Each player will also need a marker (a button or anything small) and a piece of paper.

● **1.** Divide the class into small groups.

● **2.** Give a copy of *Clothing Board Game I* to each group. Also provide each group with a die, markers, and a piece of paper. If students use a coin as a die, the class should decide which side of the coin will indicate a move of one space and which will indicate a move of two spaces.

● **3.** Have students place their markers on *Start*. The group should decide who goes first. That student begins the game by rolling the cube (or flipping the coin) and moving his or her marker. If the student responds to the question or task correctly, he or she may take one more turn. (The group decides if the response is correct.) If the student doesn't respond correctly, the next student takes a turn. No one may take more than two turns at a time.

Option 1: The first person to reach *Finish* is the winner.

Option 2: The game continues until each student reaches *Finish*. This way everybody is a winner.

8.5

NAME THAT CLOTHING ITEM! **/*
WORD CLUE GAME**
Picture Dictionary Pages 65–70

PAIRS

ACTIVITY MASTER
73

THE ACTIVITY

Pairs of students will compete against other pairs of students to guess items of clothing from clues given by their partners.

GETTING READY

Students will do this activity in pairs, competing against another pair of students. Make two copies of Activity Master 73 (*Clothing Word Clue Cards*) for each group of four students. Cut each copy of the Activity Master into separate cards.

● **1.** Divide the class into groups of four. Then divide each group into two teams—Team A and Team B.

● **2.** Give each team a set of *Clothing Word Clue Cards*.

● **3.** Have the teams shuffle the cards and place them face down in a stack.

● **4.** Tell students that the object of the game is to listen to clues from their partners to guess the item of clothing on the card. Students will sit across from their partners. The partner will give up to three clues. Each clue is worth one point. If the student isn't able to name the item, the card goes to the bottom of the pile and the pair is given three points.

The game continues until all the cards have been guessed. The team with the *least number of points* wins the game.

8.6 THE BRADY FAMILY PHOTOS **
PICTURE DIFFERENCES
Picture Dictionary Pages 71–72

**ACTIVITY MASTERS
74 & 75**

THE ACTIVITY

Students work together to find differences between two photographs of the Brady family.

GETTING READY

Students will do this activity in pairs. Make copies of Activity Master 74 (*Brady Family Photo A*) for half the class and Activity Master 75 (*Brady Family Photo B*) for the other half of the class.

● **1.** Divide the class into pairs.

● **2.** Give a copy of *Brady Family Photo A* to one member of each pair and a copy of *Brady Family Photo B* to the other.

● **3.** Ask students what clothing items they see in the pictures. Together, brainstorm a list of vocabulary and write the words on the board.

● **4.** Tell students that the object of the game is to find eight differences between the two photographs. Some differences are with the clothing items people are wearing. Other differences are with clothing problems. Do two examples before beginning the game. For example:

> In Photo A, Ben is wearing a short-sleeved shirt.
> In Photo B, Ben is wearing a long-sleeved shirt.

> In Photo A, Mary's pants are too short.
> In Photo B, Mary's pants are too long.

● **5.** When the activity is completed, call on students to tell the differences they found between the two Brady Family photos.

ANSWER KEY

In the Brady Family Photo A	In the Brady Family Photo B
Ben is wearing a short-sleeved shirt.	Ben is wearing a long-sleeved shirt.
Grandpa is wearing a striped tie.	Grandpa is wearing a plaid tie.
Grandma is wearing a V-neck sweater.	Grandma is wearing a turtleneck sweater.
Sally is wearing a polka-dotted T-shirt.	Sally is wearing a checked T-shirt.
Mary's pants are too short.	Mary's pants are too long.
Bobby's shirt is too tight.	Bobby's shirt is too baggy.
Mrs. Brady's blouse has a stained collar.	Mrs. Brady's blouse has a missing button.
Mr. Brady's jacket has a torn pocket.	Mr. Brady's jacket has a broken zipper.

8.7

CLOTHING BOARD GAME II **/*
BOARD GAME
Picture Dictionary Pages 71–73

ACTIVITY MASTERS
7, 76, & 77

THE ACTIVITY

Students play a board game that focuses on describing clothing, clothing problems and alterations, and doing the laundry.

GETTING READY

Students will do this activity in groups. Make a copy of Activity Master 76 (*Clothing Board Game II*) and Activity Master 77 (*Laundry & Alteration Cards*) for each group. Cut each copy of Activity Master 77 into separate cards.

Each group will need a die. You can duplicate Activity Master 7 (*Game Cube*) to make a die for each group, or students can use a coin. Each player will also need a marker (a button or anything small).

1. Divide the class into small groups.

2. Give a copy of *Clothing Board Game II* and a set of *Laundry & Alteration Cards* to each group. Also provide each group with a die and markers. If students use a coin as a die, the class should decide which side of the coin will indicate a move of one space and which will indicate a move of two spaces. Place the *Laundry & Alteration Cards* face down on the table in two piles—Laundry Cards and Alteration Cards.

3. Have students place their markers on *Start*. The group should decide who goes first. That student begins the game by rolling the cube (or flipping the coin) and moving his or her marker. If the student responds to the question or task correctly, he or she may take one more turn. (The group decides if the response is correct.) If the student doesn't respond correctly, the next student takes a turn.

   Option 1: The first person to reach *Finish* is the winner.

   Option 2: The game continues until each student reaches *Finish*. This way everybody is a winner.

UNIT 9

WHAT DO THEY WANT FOR THEIR BIRTHDAYS? *
INFORMATION GAP
Picture Dictionary Page 74–79

PAIRS

ACTIVITY MASTERS
78 & 79

THE ACTIVITY

Students work together to complete the Kim family birthday list.

GETTING READY

Students will do this activity in pairs. Make copies of Activity Master 78 (*Kim Family Birthday List A*) for half the class and Activity Master 79 (*Kim Family Birthday List B*) for the other half of the class.

● **1.** Divide the class into pairs.

● **2.** Give a copy of *Kim Family Birthday List A* to one member of each pair and a copy of *Kim Family Birthday List B* to the other.

● **3.** Write the following on the board for students to use as a framework for asking and answering questions:

> A. When is _____'s birthday?
> B. It's _____.
> A. What does he/she want for his/her birthday?
> B. He/She wants a/an _____.

● **4.** Tell students that each member of the pair knows the birthdays of some of the members of the Kim family and what gifts they would like. Have them ask each other questions to find out the missing information and then write the birthdays and gifts next to the correct family member.

● **5.** When the pairs have completed the activity, have them compare their birthday lists.

DEPARTMENT STORE CONCENTRATION GAME *
CONCENTRATION GAME
Picture Dictionary Pages 74–79

THE ACTIVITY

Students look for matching department store vocabulary cards.

GETTING READY

Students will do this activity in pairs. Make a copy of Activity Master 80 (*Department Store Concentration Cards*) for each pair. Cut each copy of Activity Master 80 into separate cards.

---

1. Divide the class into pairs.

2. Give a copy of *Department Store Concentration Cards* to each pair.

3. Have the pairs shuffle the cards and place them face down in three rows of six cards each.

4. Tell students that the object of the game is to find the cards that match.

5. A student turns over two cards, and if they match, that student keeps the cards. If the cards don't match, the student turns them face down and the other student takes a turn.

The play continues until all the cards have been matched. The person with the most correct *matches* wins the game.

Alternative: The game can be played in groups of four, or as a class with two competing teams.

WHAT'S IN YOUR HOME? *
CLASSROOM SEARCH
Picture Dictionary Pages 74–79

THE ACTIVITY

Students walk around the classroom asking each other about the things they have in their home.

GETTING READY

Students will do this activity as a class. Make a copy of Activity Master 81 (*What's In Your Home?*) for each student in the class.

● **1.** Give a copy of *What's in Your Home?* to each student.

● **2.** Write the following on the board for students to use as a framework for asking each other questions:

> A. Do you have _____ in your home?
> B. Yes, I do.
>   No, I don't.

● **3.** Have students walk around asking each other the question on the board. When students have found someone who has one of the items on their grids, the responding student should write his or her name in that square of the grid (only one signature is necessary for each square).

The student whose grid is filled with the most signatures is the winner of the game.

9.4 BIRTHDAY MATCH GAME **
MATCHING GAME
Picture Dictionary Pages 74–79

THE ACTIVITY

Students ask and answer questions to find someone who matches the description on their cards.

GETTING READY

Students will do this activity in groups. There are 28 cards in this activity. Divide your class into groups and use as many cards for each group as you wish.

Make two copies of Activity Master 82 (*Birthday Match Cards*) for each group. Cut each copy of the Activity Master into separate cards.

● **1.** Divide your class into groups and give each student a different *Birthday Match Card.*

● **2.** Write the following questions on the board and have students practice saying them:

> What's your name?
> When is your birthday?
> What do you want for your birthday?
> What else do you want?

● **3.** Have students circulate around the room and ask each other the questions on the board. Tell them that the object of the game is to find the one person who has the same matching information. The first pair to find their *match* is the winner.

LET'S GO SHOPPING BOARD GAME **
BOARD GAME
Picture Dictionary Pages 74–79

ACTIVITY MASTERS
7, 83, & 84

THE ACTIVITY

Students play a board game that focuses on food.

GETTING READY

Students will do this activity in groups. Make a copy of Activity Master 83 (*Let's Go Shopping Board Game*) and Activity Master 84 (*Shopping Game Mime Cards*) for each group. Cut each copy of Activity Master 84 into separate cards.

Each group will need a die. You can duplicate Activity Master 7 (*Game Cube*) to make a die for each group, or students can use a coin. Each player will also need a marker (a button or anything small).

- **1.** Divide the class into small groups.

- **2.** Give a copy of the *Let's Go Shopping Board Game* and a set of *Shopping Game Mime Cards* to each group. Also provide each group with a die and markers. If students use a coin as a die, the class should decide which side of the coin will indicate a move of one space and which will indicate a move of two spaces.

- **3.** Have students place their markers on *Start*. The group should decide who goes first. That student begins the game by rolling the cube (or flipping the coin) and moving his or her marker. If the student responds to the question or task correctly, he or she may take one more turn. (The group decides if the response is correct.) If the student doesn't respond correctly, the next student takes a turn. No one may take more than two turns at a time.

  Option 1: The first person to reach *Finish* is the winner.

  Option 2: The game continues until each student reaches *Finish*. This way everybody is a winner.

9.6

THE ACTIVITY

Students interview each other about items they would prefer to buy.

GETTING READY

Students will do this activity in pairs. Make a copy of Activity Master 85 (*Shopping Preference Survey*) for each student in the class.

● **1.** Divide the class into pairs.

● **2.** Give a copy of the *Shopping Preference Survey* to each student.

● **3.** Write the following on the board as a reference for students as they do the activity:

Would you rather buy _____ or _____?

● **4.** Have students answer the questions about themselves in column 1.

● **5.** Then have the students talk with their partners. Before they tell their partners how they answered the questions themselves, have them ask their partners the questions.

● **6.** Have students write their partners' answers in column 2 and then compare their partners' answers with their own.

● **7.** Have students report their answers and their partners' answers to the class. Encourage students to give reasons for their choices.

THE ACTIVITY

Groups discuss solutions to problem situations.

GETTING READY

Students will do this activity in groups of three. Make a copy of Activity Master 86 ("*What to Do?*" *Cards*) for each group. Cut each copy of Activity Master 86 into separate cards.

● **1.** Divide the class into groups of three.

● **2.** Give each group a set of *What to Do?* cards. Have students place the cards face down in a pile.

● **3.** Before beginning the activity, review expressions for agreeing and disagreeing. For example:

Agree Completely:
Absolutely!
Exactly!
You're right!
I totally agree with you!
I couldn't agreement with you more.

Agree a little:
You have a point there.
Well, you may be right.
Perhaps.

Disagree a little:
I'm not sure I agree with you.
That may be true, but . . .
I'm not sure about that.

Disagree strongly:
I'm afraid I disagree with you.
I disagree completely.
I couldn't disagree with you more.

● **4.** Student A picks a card and reads the problem. Student B gives advice by telling Student A what the person with the problem should do. Student C listens and reacts to Student B's advice by agreeing, or disagreeing and offering a different solution to the problem. Then all three must discuss the situation until they reach an agreement on what is the best advice. Encourage students to use the expressions for agreeing and disagreeing.

● **5.** For the next problem, Student B picks the card, Student C gives advice, and Student A reacts. Continue switching roles until all the problem situations have been discussed.

● **6.** After the groups have finished their discussions, have them present their solutions to the class.

Variation: Put students into pairs or small groups as appropriate and have students role play the situation. Where only one character is mentioned in the problem, add a friend or family member to help discuss the problem with the character.

UNIT 10

WHAT DID YOU DO AT THE BANK? *
CLASSROOM SEARCH
Picture Dictionary Pages 80–81

10.1

CLASS

ACTIVITY MASTER
87

THE ACTIVITY

Students walk around the classroom asking each other about what they did in banking and finance last month.

GETTING READY

Students will do this activity as a class. Make a copy of Activity Master 87 (*What Did You Do at the Bank?*) for each student in the class.

● **1.** Give each student a copy of *What Did You Do at the Bank?*

● **2.** Write the following on the board for students to use as a framework for asking each other questions:

> A. Did you _____ last month?
> B. Yes, I did.
>   No, I didn't.

● **3.** Have students walk around asking each other Yes/No questions about banking and finance activities they did last month. For example, "Did you make a deposit last month?" Students must answer truthfully. When students have found someone who did one of the activities on their grids, the responding student should write his or her name in that square of the grid (only one signature is necessary for each square).

The student whose grid is filled with the most signatures is the winner of the game.

10.2

AMELIA'S BUSY WEEK **/***
TELL-A-STORY
Picture Dictionary Pages 80–81

GROUPS

ACTIVITY MASTER
88

THE ACTIVITY

Groups arrange a set of pictures in any order they wish and write a story about it.

GETTING READY

Students will do this activity in groups. Make a copy of Activity Master 88 (*Amelia Story Cards*) for each group. Cut each copy of Activity Master 88 into separate cards.

● **1.** Divide the class into small groups.

● **2.** Give each group of set of *Amelia Story Cards*.

● **3.** Have each group lay out the cards and decide what order to put them in. When they have decided the order they want, have them write a story about all the banking and finance activities that Amelia either did or is going to do this week.

● **4.** When everyone has finished, have the groups take turns telling the rest of the class their story about Amelia's busy week.

BANKING & FINANCE BOARD GAME **
BOARD GAME
Picture Dictionary Pages 80–81

THE ACTIVITY

Students play a board game that focuses on banking and finances.

GETTING READY

Students will do this activity in groups. Make a copy of Activity Master 89 (*Banking & Finance Board Game*) for each group.

Each group will need a die. You can duplicate Activity Master 7 (*Game Cube*) to make a die for each group, or students can use a coin. Each player will also need a marker (a button or anything small).

- **1.** Divide the class into small groups.

- **2.** Give a copy of the *Banking & Finance Board Game* to each group. Also provide each group with a die and markers. If students use a coin as a die, the class should decide which side of the coin will indicate a move of one space and which will indicate a move of two spaces.

- **3.** Have students place their markers on *Start.* The group should decide who goes first. That student begins the game by rolling the cube (or flipping the coin) and moving his or her marker. If the student responds to the question or task correctly, he or she may take one more turn. (The group decides if the response is correct.) If the student doesn't respond correctly, the next student takes a turn. No one may take more than two turns at a time.

  Option 1: The first person to reach *Finish* is the winner.

  Option 2: The game continues until each student reaches *Finish*. This way everybody is a winner.

10.4

POST OFFICE & LIBRARY MEMORY CHALLENGE ∗∗
MEMORY GAME
Picture Dictionary Pages 82–83

PAIRS

ACTIVITY MASTERS
90 & 91

THE ACTIVITY

Students look at pairs of pictures and try to remember the differences between them.

GETTING READY

Students will do this activity in pairs. Make copies of Activity Master 90 (*They Did Different Things*) and Activity Master 91 (*Post Office & Library Memory Challenge*) for each pair.

1. Divide the class into pairs.

2. Give each pair a copy of *They Did Different Things*.

3. Tell students that they will have 3 minutes to study the pictures carefully and try to remember the differences—for example, Omar mailed a letter; Owen mailed a package. After they have studied the information, tell them to put the Activity Master aside.

4. Next give each pair a copy of *Post Office & Library Memory Challenge*. Have them work together to answer the questions based on their memory of the pictures on Activity Master 90.

5. When students have completed answering the questions, have them look at Activity Master 90 again to check their answers.

ANSWER KEY

1. a letter
2. a package
3. roll of stamps
4. sheet of stamps
5. priority mail
6. express mail
7. card catalog
8. online catalog
9. media section
10. reference section
11. books on tape
12. CDs
13. magazines
14. newspapers
15. dictionary
16. encyclopedia

DO WE DO THE SAME THINGS? **
PAIR COMPETITION
Picture Dictionary Pages 82–83

PAIRS

ACTIVITY MASTER
92

THE ACTIVITY

Pairs of students complete statements and then compete to see how similar they are.

GETTING READY

Students will do this activity in pairs. Make a copy of Activity Master 92 (*Do We Do the Same Things?*) for each student in the class.

- **1.** Divide the class into pairs.
- **2.** Give a copy of *Do We Do the Same Things?* to each student.
- **3.** Have each student circle the information in each of the statements that is true about himself or herself.
- **4.** Then have them take turns reading the statements. If their answers are the same, they earn a point. If their answers are different, they don't earn a point.
- **5.** When students have completed the statements, they should report to the class how many points they earned. The winning pair should then share their matching statements with the class. For example:

  We take our letters to the post office.
  We don't buy stamps at the post office.
  We know the name of our mail carrier.

AN UNFORTUNATE DAY IN BROOKDALE *
INFORMATION GAP
Picture Dictionary Page 85

PAIRS

ACTIVITY MASTERS
93 & 94

THE ACTIVITY

Students work together to find out what crimes and emergencies took place yesterday in the community of Brookdale.

GETTING READY

Students will do this activity in pairs. Make copies of Activity Master 93 (*Crimes and Emergencies A*) for half the class and Activity Master 94 (*Crimes and Emergencies B*) for the other half of the class.

---

1. Divide the class into pairs.

2. Give a copy of *Crimes and Emergencies A* to one member of each pair and a copy of *Crimes and Emergencies B* to the other.

3. Tell students that yesterday was a terrible day in the community of Brookdale. There were several crimes and emergencies. Student A has visual clues of some of the crimes and emergencies and Student B has visual clues of others. The goal of the activity is to find out the missing information and write it in their charts.

4. Write the following on the board for students to use as a reference as they do the activity:

   A. What happened on/at _____?
   B. There was a _____.

5. When the pairs have completed the activity, have them compare information.

COMMUNITY LIFE BOARD GAME **
BOARD GAME
Picture Dictionary Pages 82–85

THE ACTIVITY

Students play a board game that focuses on the post office, library, community institutions, and crime and emergencies.

GETTING READY

Students will do this activity in groups. Make a copy of Activity Master 95 (*Community Life Board Game*) for each group.

Each group will need a die. You can duplicate Activity Master 7 (*Game Cube*) to make a die for each group, or students can use a coin. Each player will also need a marker (a button or anything small).

● **1.** Divide the class into small groups.

● **2.** Give a copy of the *Community Life Board Game* to each group. Also provide each group with a die and markers. If students use a coin as a die, the class should decide which side of the coin will indicate a move of one space and which will indicate a move of two spaces.

● **3.** Have students place their markers on *Start*. The group should decide who goes first. That student begins the game by rolling the cube (or flipping the coin) and moving his or her marker. If the student responds to the question or task correctly, he or she may take one more turn. (The group decides if the response is correct.) If the student doesn't respond correctly, the next student takes a turn. No one may take more than two turns at a time.

Option 1: The first person to reach *Finish* is the winner.

Option 2: The game continues until each student reaches *Finish*. This way everybody is a winner.

ACTIVITY MASTERS
7 & 96

FACE RACE! *
DRAWING GAME
Picture Dictionary Pages 86–87

THE ACTIVITY

Students roll dice and draw a body part on the board based on the number they roll.

GETTING READY

Students will do this activity in teams. Make two copies of Activity Master 96 (*Face Race Drawing Cards*) and four copies of Activity Master 7 (*Game Cube*). Give one copy of the *Face Race Drawing Cards* and two die to each team.

● **1.** Divide the class into two teams.

● **2.** Give each team a copy of the *Face Race Drawing Cards* and two game cubes.

● **3.** Each team takes a turn at rolling both cubes. Based on the number they roll, a team member goes to the board and draws the body part on the card that corresponds to that number. For example, if a team rolls a "4," that team member draws a mouth on the board. Each team draws its own body. If a team rolls a number for a body part that has already been drawn, they lose their chance to draw and the other team takes its turn.

The first team to draw a complete body wins.

11.2

PARTS OF THE BODY BOARD GAME **
BOARD GAME
Picture Dictionary Pages 86–87

GROUPS

ACTIVITY MASTERS
7, 97, & 98

THE ACTIVITY

Students play a board game that focuses on the body.

GETTING READY

Students will do this activity in groups. Make a copy of Activity Master 97 (*Parts of the Body Board Game*) and Activity Master 98 (*Parts of the Body Drawing Cards*) for each group. Cut each copy of Activity Master 98 into separate cards.

Each group will need a die. You can duplicate Activity Master 7 (*Game Cube*) to make a die for each group, or students can use a coin. Each player will also need a marker (a button or anything small) and a piece of paper.

1. Divide the class into small groups.

2. Give a copy of the *Parts of the Body Board Game* and a set of *Parts of the Body Drawing Cards* to each group. Also provide each group with a die, markers, and a piece of paper. If students use a coin as a die, the class should decide which side of the coin will indicate a move of one space and which will indicate a move of two spaces.

3. Have students place their markers on *Start*. The group should decide who goes first. That student begins the game by rolling the cube (or flipping the coin) and moving his or her marker. If the student responds to the question or task correctly, he or she may take one more turn. (The group decides if the response is correct.) If the student doesn't respond correctly, the next student takes a turn. No one may take more than two turns at a time.

   Option 1: The first person to reach *Finish* is the winner.

   Option 2: The game continues until each student reaches *Finish*. This way everybody is a winner.

AILMENT & INJURY MEMORY CHALLENGE **

MEMORY GAME

Picture Dictionary Pages 88–89

**ACTIVITY MASTERS
99 & 100**

THE ACTIVITY

Students look at pairs of pictures and try to remember the differences between them.

GETTING READY

Students will do this activity in pairs. Make copies of Activity Master 99 (*These People Don't Feel Well*) and Activity Master 100 (*Ailment & Injury Memory Challenge*) for each pair.

- **1.** Divide the class into pairs.

- **2.** Give each pair a copy of *These People Don't Feel Well*.

- **3.** Tell students that they will have 3 minutes to study the pictures carefully and try to remember the differences—for example, Ronaldo has a cold; Donaldo has a cough. After they have studied the information, tell them to put the Activity Master aside.

- **4.** Next give each pair a copy of *Ailment & Injury Memory Challenge*. Have them work together to answer the questions based on their memory of the pictures on Activity Master 99.

- **5.** When students have completed answering the questions, have them look at Activity Master 99 again to check their answers.

ANSWER KEY

1. cold / cough
2. earache / toothache
3. swollen / itchy
4. bloated / congested
5. leg / arm
6. headache / stomachache
7. mumps / measles
8. frostbite / heatstroke
9. hiccups / chills
10. elbow / ankle

11.4

MAX MILLER'S MEDICAL HISTORY *
INFORMATION GAP
Picture Dictionary Pages 90–91

PAIRS

ACTIVITY MASTERS
101 & 102

THE ACTIVITY

Students work together to complete Max Miller's medical history.

GETTING READY

Students will do this activity in pairs. Make copies of Activity Master 101 (*Max Miller's Medical History A*) for half the class and Activity Master 102 (*Max Miller's Medical History B*) for the other half of the class.

- **1.** Divide the class into pairs.

- **2.** Give a copy of *Max Miller's Medical History A* to one member of each pair and a copy of *Max Miller's Medical History B* to the other.

- **3.** Tell students that each member of the pair knows different information about the illnesses and medical emergencies in Max Miller's life.

- **4.** Write the following on the board for students to use as a reference as they do the activity:

  > A. What happened to Max when he was _____ years old?
  > B. He had/got _____.

- **5.** When the pairs have completed the activity, have them compare their medical history forms.

WHAT SHOULD THEY DO? ***
GROUP DISCUSSION
Picture Dictionary Pages 90–91

ACTIVITY MASTER
103

THE ACTIVITY

Groups discuss solutions to problem situations.

GETTING READY

Students will do this activity in groups of three. Make a copy of Activity Master 103 (*What Should They Do?*) for each group. Cut each copy of Activity Master 103 into separate cards.

- **1.** Divide the class into groups of three.
- **2.** Give each group a set of *What Should They Do?* cards. Have students place the cards face down in a pile.
- **3.** Student A picks a card and reads the problem. Student B gives advice by telling Student A what the person with the problem should do. Student C listens and reacts to Student B's advice by agreeing, or disagreeing and offering a different solution to the problem. Then all three must discuss the situation until they reach an agreement on what is the best advice.
- **4.** For the next problem, Student B picks the card, Student C gives advice, and Student A reacts. Continue switching roles until all the problem situations have been discussed.
- **5.** After the groups have finished their discussions, have them present their solutions to the class.

11.6 MEDICAL MATCH GAME **
MATCHING GAME
Picture Dictionary Pages 92–95

GROUPS

ACTIVITY MASTER
104

THE ACTIVITY

Students try to find the person who has matching information.

GETTING READY

Students will do this activity in groups. There are 32 cards in this activity. Divide your class into groups and use as many cards for each group as you wish.

Make two copies of Activity Master 104 (*Medical Match Cards*) for each group. Cut each copy of the Activity Master into separate cards.

● **1.** Divide your class into groups and give each student a different *Medical Match Card*.

● **2.** Write the following questions on the board and have students practice saying them:

> Where were you?
> What did the doctor/dentist do?
> What did the doctor/dentist tell you?

● **3.** Have students circulate around the room asking questions based on the model on the board. Tell them that the object of the game is to find the one person who has the same matching information. The first pair to find their *match* is the winner.

MEDICAL TREATMENT BOARD GAME **
BOARD GAME
Picture Dictionary Pages 92–95

ACTIVITY MASTERS
7 & 105

THE ACTIVITY

Students play a board game that focuses on medical treatment.

GETTING READY

Students will do this activity in groups. Make a copy of Activity Master 105 (*Medical Treatment Board Game*) for each group.

Each group will need a die. You can duplicate Activity Master 7 (*Game Cube*) to make a die for each group, or students can use a coin. Each player will also need a marker (a button or anything small).

---

1. Divide the class into small groups.

2. Give a copy of the *Medical Treatment Board Game* to each group. Also provide each group with a die and markers. If students use a coin as a die, the class should decide which side of the coin will indicate a move of one space and which will indicate a move of two spaces.

3. Have students place their markers on *Start*. The group should decide who goes first. That student begins the game by rolling the cube (or flipping the coin) and moving his or her marker. If the student responds to the question or task correctly, he or she may take one more turn. (The group decides if the response is correct.) If the student doesn't respond correctly, the next student takes a turn. No one may take more than two turns at a time.

Option 1: The first person to reach *Finish* is the winner.

Option 2: The game continues until each student reaches *Finish*. This way everybody is a winner.

MEDICAL TREATMENT MEMORY CHALLENGE **
MEMORY GAME
Picture Dictionary Pages 96–97

PAIRS

ACTIVITY MASTERS
106 & 107

THE ACTIVITY

Students look at pairs of pictures and try to remember the differences between them.

GETTING READY

Students will do this activity in pairs. Make copies of Activity Master 106 (*These People Are Having Medical Treatment*) and Activity Master 107 (*Medical Treatment Memory Challenge*) for each pair.

- **1.** Divide the class into pairs.

- **2.** Give each pair a copy of *These People Are Having Medical Treatment*.

- **3.** Tell students that they will have 3 minutes to study the pictures carefully and try to remember the differences—for example, Boris is at the cardiologist. He's having blood tests; Morris is at the allergist. He's having allergy tests. After they have studied the information, tell them to put the Activity Master aside.

- **4.** Next give each pair a copy of *Medical Treatment Memory Challenge*. Have them work together to answer the questions based on their memory of the pictures on Activity Master 106.

- **5.** When students have completed answering the questions, have them look at Activity Master 106 again to check their answers.

ANSWER KEY

1. cardiologist / blood
2. allergist / allergy
3. doctor's office / nurse
4. hospital / doctor
5. operating room / surgery
6. radiology department / X-rays
7. physical therapist / physical therapy
8. audiologist / a hearing test
9. acupuncturist / acupuncture
10. counselor / counseling

DID YOU BRUSH YOUR HAIR TODAY? *
CLASSROOM SEARCH
Picture Dictionary Pages 98–100

ACTIVITY MASTER
108

THE ACTIVITY

Students walk around the classroom asking each other about personal hygiene and baby care activities.

GETTING READY

Students will do this activity as a class. Make a copy of Activity Master 108 (*Did You Brush Your Hair Today?*) for each student in the class.

- **1.** Give a copy of *Did You Brush Your Hair Today?* to each student.

- **2.** Write the following on the board for students to use as a framework for asking each other questions:

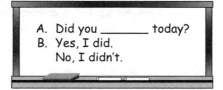

A. Did you _____ today?
B. Yes, I did.
No, I didn't.

- **3.** Have students walk around asking each other the question on the board. When students have found someone who did one of the activities on their grids, the responding student should write his or her name in that square of the grid (only one signature is necessary for each square).

  The student whose grid is filled with the most signatures is the winner of the game.

  WHAT'S YOUR FAVORITE SUBJECT? *
CLASSROOM SEARCH
Picture Dictionary Pages 101–104

ACTIVITY MASTER
109

THE ACTIVITY

Students walk around the classroom asking each other about school subjects and extracurricular activities.

GETTING READY

Students will do this activity as a class. Make a copy of Activity Master 109 (*What's Your Favorite Subject?*) for each student in the class.

● **1.** Give a copy of *What's Your Favorite Subject?* to each student.

● **2.** Write the following on the board for students to use as a framework for asking each other questions:

> A. Is/Was your favorite subject _____?
> B. Yes, it is./Yes, it was.
>   No, it isn't./No, it wasn't.
>
> A. Do you _____?/Did you _____?
> B. Yes, I do./Yes, I did.
>   No, I don't./No, I didn't.

● **3.** Have students walk around asking each other the questions on the board. (If students are still in school, they would answer in the present tense. If they are no longer in school, they would answer in the past tense.) When students find someone who answers positively to one of the questions on their grids, the responding student should write his or her name in that square of the grid (only one signature is necessary for each square).

The student whose grid is filled with the most signatures is the winner of the game.

68

AT SCHOOL BOARD GAME *
BOARD GAME
Picture Dictionary Pages 101–104

THE ACTIVITY

Students play a board game that focuses on school, school subjects, and extracurricular activities.

GETTING READY

Students will do this activity in groups. Make a copy of Activity Master 110 (*At School Board Game*) for each group.

Each group will need a die. You can duplicate Activity Master 7 (*Game Cube*) to make a die for each group, or students can use a coin. Each player will also need a marker (a button or anything small) and a piece of paper.

- **1.** Divide the class into small groups.

- **2.** Give a copy of the *At School Board Game* to each group. Also provide each group with a die, markers, and a piece of paper. If students use a coin as a die, the class should decide which side of the coin will indicate a move of one space and which will indicate a move of two spaces.

- **3.** Have students place their markers on *Start*. The group should decide who goes first. That student begins the game by rolling the cube (or flipping the coin) and moving his or her marker. If the student responds to the question or task correctly, he or she may take one more turn. (The group decides if the response is correct.) If the student doesn't respond correctly, the next student takes a turn. No one may take more than two turns at a time.

  Option 1: The first person to reach *Finish* is the winner.

  Option 2: The game continues until each student reaches *Finish*. This way everybody is a winner.

SCHOOL SUBJECT MATCH GAME *
MATCHING GAME
Picture Dictionary Pages 105–111

THE ACTIVITY

Students match key words with their corresponding school subject categories.

GETTING READY

Students will do this activity as a class. Make a copy of Activity Master 111 (*School Subject Match Cards*). Cut the Activity Master into separate cards and give a card to each student.

● **1.** Give each student a card. Half the students will have school subject category cards (for example, ARITHMETIC, PLANETS, TYPES OF LAND), and the other half will have key words that *match* each category.

● **2.** Have students walk around saying the lines on their cards until they find their school subject category match.

● **3.** When students have found their matches, have them present them to the class. For example:

    A. Jupiter, Mars, Saturn.
    B. Planets.

    A. Noun, verb, adjective.
    B. Parts of Speech.

12.4 SCHOOL SUBJECT CONCENTRATION GAME *

CONCENTRATION GAME

Picture Dictionary Pages 105–111

**ACTIVITY MASTER
112**

THE ACTIVITY

Students look for key words and their corresponding school subject categories.

GETTING READY

Students will do this activity in groups. Make a copy of Activity Master 112 (*School Subject Concentration Cards*) for each group. Cut each copy of Activity Master 112 into separate cards.

● **1.** Divide the class into groups of four. Then divide each group into two teams—Team A and Team B.

● **2.** Give each group a set of *School Subject Concentration Cards*.

● **3.** Have the groups shuffle the cards and place them face down in five rows of four cards each.

● **4.** Tell students that the object of the game is to find cards that match.

● **5.** A student from Team A turns over two cards, and if they match, that team keeps the cards. If the cards don't match, the student turns them face down and a member of Team B takes a turn.

   The play continues until all the cards have been matched. The team with the most correct *matches* wins the game.

   Alternative: This game can be played in pairs, or as a class with two competing teams.

SCHOOL SUBJECT BOARD GAME **
BOARD GAME
Picture Dictionary Pages 105–111

ACTIVITY MASTERS
7 & 113

THE ACTIVITY

Students play a board game that focuses on Math, English, Geography, Science, and the Universe.

GETTING READY

Students will do this activity in groups. Make a copy of Activity Master 113 (*School Subject Board Game*).

Each group will need a die. You can duplicate Activity Master 7 (*Game Cube*) to make a die for each group, or students can use a coin. Each player will also need a marker (a button or anything small) and a piece of paper.

⬤ **1.** Divide the class into small groups.

⬤ **2.** Give a copy of the *School Subject Board Game* to each group. Also provide each group with a die, markers, and a piece of paper. If students use a coin as a die, the class should decide which side of the coin will indicate a move of one space and which will indicate a move of two spaces.

⬤ **3.** Have students place their markers on *Start*. The group should decide who goes first. That student begins the game by rolling the cube (or flipping the coin) and moving his or her marker. If the student responds to the question or task correctly, he or she may take one more turn. (The group decides if the response is correct.) If the student doesn't respond correctly, the next student takes a turn. No one may take more than two turns at a time.

Option 1: The first person to reach *Finish* is the winner.

Option 2: The game continues until each student reaches *Finish*. This way everybody is a winner.

UNIT 13

WHAT'S MY OCCUPATION? **
LISTENING GRID
Picture Dictionary Pages 112–117

ACTIVITY MASTERS
32 & 114

THE ACTIVITY

Students place pictures on a grid and then turn them over based on sentences they hear.

GETTING READY

Students will do this activity as a class. Make a copy of Activity Master 32 (*Listening Grid*) and Activity Master 114 (*Occupation Cards*) for each student. Cut each copy of Activity Master 114 into separate cards.

● **1.** Give each student a *Listening Grid* and a set of *Occupation Cards*.

● **2.** Tell students to choose nine of the cards and place them on the grid, face up, in any order they wish.

● **3.** Say the following sentences in random order and tell students to turn over any card that you have described:

> I fix cars.
> I type and file.
> I assist patients.
> I design buildings.
> I fly an airplane.
> I grow vegetables.
> I guard buildings.
> I repair things.
> I sell things in a department store.
> I serve food.
> I supervise people.
> I take inventory in a store.
> I use a cash register.
> I assemble components.
> I take photographs.

● **4.** The first person to have three turned-over cards in a straight line—either vertically, horizontally, or diagonally—wins the game. Have the winner call out the sentences to check accuracy.

NAME THAT JOB! **/***
WORD CLUE GAME
Picture Dictionary Pages 112–117

PAIRS

ACTIVITY MASTER
115

THE ACTIVITY

Pairs of students will compete against other pairs of students to guess occupation clues given by their partners.

GETTING READY

Students will do this activity in pairs, competing against another pair of students. Make two copies of Activity Master 115 (*Occupation Word Clue Cards*) for each group of four students. Cut each copy of the Activity Master into separate cards.

1. Divide the class into groups of four. Then divide each group into two teams—Team A and Team B.

2. Give each team a set of *Occupation Word Clue Cards*.

3. Have the teams shuffle the cards and place them face down in a stack.

4. Tell students that the object of the game is to listen to clues from their partners to guess the occupation on the card. Students will sit across from their partners. The partner will give up to three clues. Each clue is worth one point. If the student isn't able to name the occupation, the card goes to the bottom of the pile and the pair is given three points.

    The game continues until all the cards have been guessed. The team with the *least number of points* wins the game.

13.3 FIND THE RIGHT EMPLOYEE! *
MATCHING GAME
Picture Dictionary Page 118

THE ACTIVITY

Student *employers* try to find matching *employees*.

GETTING READY

Students will do this activity in groups. There are 32 cards in this activity. Divide the class into groups and use as many cards for each group as you wish.

Make two copies of Activity Master 116 (*Employer/Employee Match Cards*) for each group. Cut each Activity Master into separate cards.

● **1.** Divide the class into groups and give each student an *Employer/Employee Match Card*. Some students will receive employer cards, and others will receive employee cards. The employer cards have a series of statements about the type of employee they are looking for. The employee cards have information about the employee's experience and the type of job that person is applying for.

● **2.** Write the following on the board for students to use as a framework for asking and answering questions:

> A. Can you work _____?
>   Can you _____?
> B. Yes, I can.
>   No, I can't.
>
> A. Do you want a job as a/an _____?
> B. Yes, I do.
>   No, I don't.

● **3.** Have students circulate around the room asking and answering questions based on the model on the board. For example:

> Can you work Monday through Friday?/Can you work evenings?
> Can you work from 8:00 A.M. to 4:00 P.M.?/Can you work part-time?
> Can you use a computer?
> Do you want a job as a secretary?

Tell students that the object of the game is for each *employer* to find the one *employee* who has the same matching information. The first pair to find their match is the winner.

13.4

THE BEST ONE FOR THE JOB! ***
GROUP DISCUSSION
Picture Dictionary Page 118

GROUPS

ACTIVITY MASTER
117

THE ACTIVITY

Groups evaluate five people based on their experience and skills to determine who would be the best receptionist in an international law office.

GETTING READY

Students will do this activity in groups. Make a copy of Activity Master 117 (*The Best One for the Job!*) for each student in the class.

- **1.** Divide the class into groups.
- **2.** Give each student a copy of *The Best One for the Job!*
- **3.** Tell students that these five people are applying for a job as a receptionist in an international law office. Each group should decide which person they think would be the best receptionist based on that person's experience and skills.
- **4.** After the groups have made their decisions, have them explain their reasons to the class.

A BUSY DAY AT WORK **
INFORMATION GAP
Picture Dictionary Pages 119–120

THE ACTIVITY

Students role-play a situation in which a supervisor is asking an office assistant about the completion of several tasks.

GETTING READY

Students will do this activity in pairs. Make copies of Activity Master 118 (*Employee Checklist*) for half the class and Activity Master 119 (*Supervisor Checklist*) for the other half of the class.

● **1.** Divide the class into pairs. Tell students that this is a role-playing activity in which one student is an assistant in a small office and the other is the supervisor.

● **2.** Give a copy of the *Employee Checklist* to one member of each pair and a copy of the *Supervisor Checklist* to the other.

● **3.** Explain that both the employee and the supervisor have a list of tasks at work. Before beginning the activity, tell the employees to put a check before the tasks they completed and leave the others blank.

● **4.** Write the following on the board for students to use as a framework while doing the activity:

> A. Did you _____?
> B. Yes, I did. I _____ a little while ago.
>
> A. Did you _____?
> B. No, I didn't. I'll _____ in a little while.

● **5.** Have the pairs role-play the situation based on the models on the board. For example:

> (If the employer put a check before "sweep the coat closet" on the checklist:)
> A. Did you sweep the coat closet yet?
> B. Yes, I did. I swept the coat closet a little while ago.
>
> (If the employee left the rule blank before "fix the coat rack":)
> A. Did you fix the coat rack yet?
> B. No, I didn't. I'll fix the coat rack in a little while.

● **6.** When the role play is complete, have the *employers* and *employees* compare their checklists to see if they match.

OFFICE SUPPLY MEMORY GAME **
MEMORY GAME
Picture Dictionary Page 121

THE ACTIVITY

Students look at office supplies on someone's desk for two minutes and then try to remember the items they saw.

GETTING READY

Students will do this activity as a class. Make copies of Activity Master 120 (*Diego's Desk*) and Activity Master 121 (*What I Remember About Diego's Desk*) for each student.

● **1.** Give each student a copy of *Diego's Desk*.

● **2.** Tell students that they will have 2 minutes to study the picture carefully and try to remember all the items on Diego's desk. After they have studied the information, tell them to put the Activity Master aside.

● **3.** Next, give each student a copy of *What I Remember About Diego's Desk*. The first person to complete the Activity Master should raise his or her hand and read the list to the class. If the items are correct, that student is the winner of the game. If not, the first student to correctly identify all the items wins.

ANSWER KEY

appointment book
clipboard
desk calendar
desk pad
electric pencil sharpener
envelope
glue
letter tray
note pad
rotary card file
rubber band
stapler

13.7

ON THE JOB SITE **
LISTENING GRID
Picture Dictionary Pages 121–123

ACTIVITY MASTERS
32 & 122

THE ACTIVITY

Students place pictures on a grid and then turn them over based on sentences they hear.

GETTING READY

Students will do this activity as a class. Make a copy of Activity Master 32 (*Listening Grid*) and Activity Master 122 (*Job Site Cards*) for each student. Cut each copy of Activity Master 122 into separate cards.

---

1. Give each student a *Listening Grid* and a set of *Job Site Cards*.

2. Tell students to choose nine of the cards and place them on the grid, face up, in any order they wish.

3. Say the following sentences in random order and tell students to turn over any card that you have described:

   You use this when you come into work and when you leave work.
   You put your suggestions in this.
   Factory workers put their clothes here when they come to work.
   You assemble things on this at a factory.
   This is where you get your paychecks.
   You drill with this.
   You measure things with this.
   You wear this on your head for safety.
   You wear this on your body for safety.
   You wear these in your ears for safety.
   You wear these over your eyes for safety.
   You wear these on your feet for safety.
   You put this over your nose and mouth for safety.
   This sign means "flammable."
   This sign means "poisonous."
   This sign means "radioactive."
   This sign means "biohazard."
   This sign means "electrical hazard."
   Use this if there's a fire at the workplace.
   You put first-aid supplies in this.

4. The first person to have three turned-over cards in a straight line—either vertically, horizontally, or diagonally—wins the game. Have the winner call out the sentences to check accuracy.

 **WORKPLACE BOARD GAME** **

BOARD GAME

Picture Dictionary Pages 112–123

ACTIVITY MASTERS
7 & 123

THE ACTIVITY

Students play a board game that focuses on the workplace.

GETTING READY

Students will do this activity in groups. Make a copy of Activity Master 123 (*Workplace Board Game*) for each group.

Each group will need a die. You can duplicate Activity Master 7 (*Game Cube*) to make a die for each group, or students can use a coin. Each player will also need a marker (a button or anything small).

● **1.** Divide the class into small groups.

● **2.** Give a copy of the *Workplace Board Game* to each group. Also provide each group with a die and markers. If students use a coin as a die, the class should decide which side of the coin will indicate a move of one space and which will indicate a move of two spaces.

● **3.** Have students place their markers on *Start*. The group should decide who goes first. That student begins the game by rolling the cube (or flipping the coin) and moving his or her marker. If the student responds to the question or task correctly, he or she may take one more turn. (The group decides if the response is correct.) If the student doesn't respond correctly, the next student takes a turn. No one may take more than two turns at a time.

Option 1: The first person to reach *Finish* is the winner.

Option 2: The game continues until each student reaches *Finish*. This way everybody is a winner.

  14.1 **TRANSPORTATION MATCH GAME ***
MATCHING GAME
Picture Dictionary Pages 124–125

GROUPS
ACTIVITY MASTER
124

THE ACTIVITY

Students try to find the person who has matching information.

GETTING READY

Students will do this activity in groups. There are 32 cards in this activity. Divide your class into groups and use as many cards for each group as you wish.

Make two copies of Activity Master 124 (*Transportation Match Cards*) for each group. Cut each Activity Master into separate cards.

● **1.** Divide the class into groups and give each student a *Transportation Match Card*.

● **2.** Write the following questions and answers on the board and have students practice saying them:

> A. How do you get to English class?
> How do you get to the mall?
> How do you get to the park?
> How do you get to the supermarket?
> B. I take the bus.
> I take the train.
> I ride my bicycle.
> I drive my S.U.V.

● **3.** Have students circulate around the room asking and answering questions based on the model on the board. Tell them that the object of the game is to find the one person who has the matching information. The first pair to find their *match* is the winner.

14.2

WHAT'S THE CAR PART? **
LISTENING GRID
Picture Dictionary Pages 126–127

ACTIVITY MASTERS
32 & 125

THE ACTIVITY

Students place pictures on a grid and then turn them over based on sentences they hear.

GETTING READY

Students will do this activity as a class. Make a copy of Activity Master 32 (*Listening Grid*) and Activity Master 125 (*Car Part Cards*) for each student. Cut each copy of Activity Master 125 into separate cards.

● **1.** Give each student a *Listening Grid* and a set of *Car Part Cards*.

● **2.** Tell students to choose nine of the cards and place them on the grid, face up, in any order they wish.

● **3.** Say the following sentences in random order and tell students to turn over any card that you have described:

> This goes on the top of your car. You can put things on this.
> This is a computer in your car that gives you directions to get places.
> This is a cover for your wheel.
> This is a part of the roof of your car that opens up.
> This is rubber. It goes over your wheel. Every car has four of these.
> This is something on your dashboard that you can put things in.
> This opens up and protects you if you hit another car.
> This shows how fast your car is going.
> You look through this to see cars behind you.
> You use these to start your car battery.
> You use these when it rains.
> You use this to lift your car when you have a flat tire.
> You use this to shift gears.
> Your car radio needs this.
> This shows your car registration number. You put it on the back, and sometimes on the front of your car.

● **4.** The first person to have three turned-over cards in a straight line—either vertically, horizontally, or diagonally—wins the game. Have the winner call out the sentences to check accuracy.

14.3 TRANSPORTATION BOARD GAME **
BOARD GAME
Picture Dictionary Pages 124–127, 130

ACTIVITY MASTERS
7, 126, & 127

THE ACTIVITY

Students play a board game that focuses on types of transportation.

GETTING READY

Students will do this activity in groups. Make a copy of Activity Master 126 (*Transportation Board Game*) and Activity Master 127 (*Traffic Sign Cards*) for each group. Cut each copy of Activity Master 127 into separate cards.

Each group will need a die. You can duplicate Activity Master 7 (*Game Cube*) to make a die for each group, or students can use a coin. Each player will also need a marker (a button or anything small) and a piece of paper.

● **1.** Divide the class into small groups.

● **2.** Give a copy of the *Transportation Board Game* and a set of *Traffic Sign Cards* to each group. Also provide each group with a die, markers, and a piece of paper. If students use a coin as a die, the class should decide which side of the coin will indicate a move of one space and which will indicate a move of two spaces.

● **3.** Have students place their markers on *Start*. The group should decide who goes first. That student begins the game by rolling the cube (or flipping the coin) and moving his or her marker. If the student responds to the question or task correctly, he or she may take one more turn. (The group decides if the response is correct.) If the student doesn't respond correctly, the next student takes a turn. No one may take more than two turns at a time.

Option 1: The first person to reach *Finish* is the winner.

Option 2: The game continues until each student reaches *Finish*. This way everybody is a winner.

WHAT'S DIFFERENT ABOUT THESE HIGHWAYS? **

14.4

PICTURE DIFFERENCES

Picture Dictionary Pages 125, 128

THE ACTIVITY

Students work together to find differences between two highways.

GETTING READY

Students will do this activity in pairs. Make copies of Activity 128 (*Interstate 70*) for half the class and Activity Master 129 (*Interstate 99*) for the other half of the class.

- **1.** Divide the class into pairs.

- **2.** Give a copy of *Interstate 70* to one member of each pair and a copy of *Interstate 99* to the other.

- **3.** Tell students that the object of the game is to find seven differences between the two highways. Do one example before beginning the game. For example:

  On Interstate 70, a car is going over a bridge.
  On Interstate 99, a truck is going over a bridge.

- **4.** When the activity is completed, call on students to tell the differences they found between the two highways.

ANSWER KEY

On Interstate 70	On Interstate 99
A car is going over a bridge.	A truck is going over a bridge.
A bus is going through a tunnel.	A motorcycle is going through a tunnel.
A convertible is at a tollbooth.	A jeep is at a tollbooth.
There are three cars in the middle lane.	There are two cars in the middle lane.
The speed limit is 15 miles per hour.	The speed limit is 10 miles per hour.
The exit sign is Exit 2.	The exit sign is Exit 4.
One car is on the exit ramp.	Two cars are on the exit ramp.

14.5   AIRPLANE & HOTEL BOARD GAME **
BOARD GAME
Picture Dictionary Pages 131–133

THE ACTIVITY

Students play a board game that focuses on air travel and hotels.

GETTING READY

Students will do this activity in groups. Make a copy of Activity Master 130 (*Airplane & Hotel Board Game*) for each group.

Each group will need a die. You can duplicate Activity Master 7 (*Game Cube*) to make a die for each group, or students can use a coin. Each player will also need a marker (a button or anything small).

● **1.** Divide the class into small groups.

● **2.** Give a copy of the *Airplane & Hotel Board Game* to each group. Also provide each group with a die and markers. If students use a coin as a die, the class should decide which side of the coin will indicate a move of one space and which will indicate a move of two spaces.

● **3.** Have students place their markers on *Start*. The group should decide who goes first. That student begins the game by rolling the cube (or flipping the coin) and moving his or her marker. If the student responds to the question or task correctly, he or she may take one more turn. (The group decides if the response is correct.) If the student doesn't respond correctly, the next student takes a turn. No one may take more than two turns at a time.

Option 1: The first person to reach *Finish* is the winner.

Option 2: The game continues until each student reaches *Finish*. This way everybody is a winner.

14.6

ROBERTO TOOK A TRIP **/***
TELL-A-STORY
Picture Dictionary Pages 131–133

ACTIVITY MASTER
131

THE ACTIVITY

Groups arrange a set of pictures in any order they wish and write a story about it.

GETTING READY

Students will do this activity in groups. Make a copy of Activity Master 131 (*Roberto Story Cards*) for each group. Cut each copy of Activity Master 131 into separate cards.

- **1.** Divide the class into small groups.
- **2.** Give each group of set of *Roberto Story Cards*.
- **3.** Have each group lay out the cards and decide what order to put them in. When they have decided the order they want, have them write a story about Roberto's trip.
- **4.** When everyone has finished, have the groups take turns telling the rest of the class their story about Roberto's trip.

 UNIT **15**

  15.1

WHAT DO YOU LIKE TO DO IN YOUR FREE TIME? *
CLASSROOM SEARCH
Picture Dictionary Pages 134–136

CLASS

ACTIVITY MASTER
132

THE ACTIVITY

Students walk around the classroom asking each other about the kinds of hobbies, crafts, and games they like, as well as places they like to go to during their free time.

GETTING READY

Students will do this activity as a class. Make a copy of Activity Master 132 (*What Do You Like to Do in Your Free Time?*) for each student in the class.

● **1.** Give a copy of *What Do You Like to Do in Your Free Time?* to each student. Ask them to think about their favorite hobbies, crafts, and games.

● **2.** Write the following on the board for student reference during the activity:

Do you like to _____?

● **3.** Have students walk around asking each other the question on the board. When students have found someone who likes to do one of the activities on their grids, the responding student should write his or her name in that square of the grid (only one signature is necessary for each square).

The student whose grid is filled with the most signatures is the winner of the game.

WHAT'S THE RECREATION ITEM? **
LISTENING GRID
Picture Dictionary Pages 137–141

THE ACTIVITY

Students place pictures on a grid and then turn them over based on sentences they hear.

GETTING READY

Students will do this activity as a class. Make a copy of Activity Master 32 (*Listening Grid*) and Activity Master 133 (*Recreation Cards*) for each student. Cut each copy of Activity Master 133 into separate cards.

● **1.** Give each student a *Listening Grid* and a set of *Recreation Cards*.

● **2.** Tell students to choose nine of the cards and place them on the grid, face up, in any order they wish.

● **3.** Say the following sentences in random order and tell students to turn over any card that you have described:

> We use this to cook our food in the park.
> I sit on this when I go to the park.
> My children love to ride on this.
> My children like to climb on this.
> I sit on this at the beach.
> I wear this when I go to the beach.
> I put sand and water in this when I'm at the beach.
> We put food and drinks in this when we go to the beach.
> We sleep in this when we go camping.
> This tells me directions when I go hiking.
> I wear these when I go rollerblading.
> We put food in this when we have a picnic.
> I always wear this when I ride my mountain bike.
> I wear these when I play racquetball.
> I use this when I play tennis.
> I use this when I do gymnastics.

● **4.** The first person to have three turned-over cards in a straight line—either vertically, horizontally, or diagonally—wins the game. Have the winner call out the sentences to check accuracy.

WHAT'S DIFFERENT ABOUT THESE BEACHES? *
PICTURE DIFFERENCES
Picture Dictionary Page 138

PAIRS

ACTIVITY MASTERS
134 & 135

THE ACTIVITY

Students work together to find differences between two beaches.

GETTING READY

Students will do this activity in pairs. Make copies of Activity Master 134 (*The Surfside Beach*) for half the class and Activity Master 135 (*The Bayside Beach*) for the other half of the class.

- **1.** Divide the class into pairs.

- **2.** Give a copy of *The Surfside Beach* to one member of each pair and a copy of *The Bayside Beach* to the other.

- **3.** Tell students that the object of the game is to find eight differences between the two beaches. Do one example before beginning the game. For example:

    At the Surfside Beach, a boy is flying a kite.
    At the Bayside Beach, a girl is flying a kite.

- **4.** When the activity is completed, call on students to tell the differences they found between the two beaches.

ANSWER KEY

At the Surfside Beach	**At the Bayside Beach**
A boy is flying a kite.	A girl is flying a kite.
The lifeguard is a woman.	The lifeguard is a man.
The beach umbrella is striped.	The beach umbrella is polka-dotted.
The sunbather is wearing sunglasses.	The sunbather isn't wearing sunglasses.
A boy is holding a surfboard.	A girl is holding a surfboard.
A girl is holding a pail.	A girl is holding a shovel.
The shovel is on the sand.	The pail is on the sand.
A mother is putting sunscreen on her daughter.	A father is putting sunscreen on his son.

RECREATION BOARD GAME **
BOARD GAME
Picture Dictionary Pages 137–141

**ACTIVITY MASTERS
7 & 136**

THE ACTIVITY

Students play a board game that focuses on recreation and individual sports.

GETTING READY

Students will do this activity in groups. Make a copy of Activity Master 136 (*Recreation Board Game*) for each group.

Each group will need a die. You can duplicate Activity Master 7 (*Game Cube*) to make a die for each group, or students can use a coin. Each player will also need a marker (a button or anything small).

---

1. Divide the class into small groups.

2. Give a copy of the *Recreation Board Game* to each group. Also provide each group with a die and markers. If students use a coin as a die, the class should decide which side of the coin will indicate a move of one space and which will indicate a move of two spaces.

3. Have students place their markers on *Start*. The group should decide who goes first. That student begins the game by rolling the cube (or flipping the coin) and moving his or her marker. If the student responds to the question or task correctly, he or she may take one more turn. (The group decides if the response is correct.) If the student doesn't respond correctly, the next student takes a turn. No one may take more than two turns at a time.

   Option 1: The first person to reach *Finish* is the winner.

   Option 2: The game continues until each student reaches *Finish*. This way everybody is a winner.

15.5  RECREATION RACE **
GROUP COMPETITION
Picture Dictionary Pages 137–141

GROUPS

ACTIVITY MASTER
137

THE ACTIVITY

Teams compete to identify types of recreation based on clues.

GETTING READY

Students will do this activity in groups. Make a copy of Activity Master 137 (*Recreation Race*) for each group. You will also need a watch with a second hand or a timer for this activity.

- **1.** Divide the class into small groups.

- **2.** Give each group of copy of *Recreation Race* and tell them NOT to turn it over until you instruct them to do so.

- **3.** Begin timing the activity. Tell students to turn over the Activity Master and work together to identify the type of recreation based on the clues.

- **4.** The first group to complete the *Recreation Race* should raise their hands and tell their answers. If all the answers are correct, that group is the winner. If any answer is incorrect, the first group to identify the correct answer is the winner.

ANSWER KEY

Clue: You need a bow and arrow and a target for this activity.
Answer: archery

Clue: You need a racket and birdie for this activity.
Answer: badminton

Clue: You need goggles and a racket for this activity.
Answer: racquetball

Clue: You need a flying disc for this activity.
Answer: Frisbee

Clue: You need gloves and trunks for this activity.
Answer: boxing

Clue: You need a saddle, reins, and stirrups for this activity.
Answer: horseback riding

Clue: You need a uniform and mat for this activity.
Answer: wrestling

Clue: You need a sleeping bag, tent, and lantern for this activity.
Answer: camping

Clue: You need a compass and trail map for this activity.
Answer: hiking

Clue: You need a harness and rope for this activity.
Answer: rock climbing

Clue: You need a blanket and thermos for this activity.
Answer: a picnic

Clue: You need barbells and weights for this activity.
Answer: weightlifting

15.6

SPORT & EXERCISE ACTION BOARD GAME **
BOARD GAME
Picture Dictionary Pages 142–146

GROUPS

ACTIVITY MASTERS
7, 138, 139, & 140

THE ACTIVITY

Students play a board game that focuses on sports and exercise actions.

GETTING READY

Students will do this activity in groups. Make a copy of Activity Master 138 (*Sport & Exercise Action Board Game*), Activity Master 139 (*Sport & Exercise Action Cards*), and Activity Master 140 (*Finish-the-Sentence Cards*) for each group. Cut each copy of Activity Masters 139 and 140 into separate cards.

Each group will need a die. You can duplicate Activity Master 7 (*Game Cube*) to make a die for each group, or students can use a coin. Each player will also need a marker (a button or anything small).

- **1.** Divide the class into small groups.
- **2.** Give a copy of the *Sport & Exercise Action Board Game* and a set of *Sport & Exercise Action Cards* and *Finish-the-Sentence Cards* to each group. Also provide each group with a die and markers. If students use a coin as a die, the class should decide which side of the coin will indicate a move of one space and which will indicate a move of two spaces.
- **3.** Have students place their markers on *Start*. The group should decide who goes first. That student begins the game by rolling the cube (or flipping the coin) and moving his or her marker. If the student responds to the question or task correctly, he or she may take one more turn. (The group decides if the response is correct.) If the student doesn't respond correctly, the next student takes a turn. No one may take more than two turns at a time.

  Option 1: The first person to reach *Finish* is the winner.

  Option 2: The game continues until each student reaches *Finish*. This way everybody is a winner.

GUESS THE SPORT! **/***
TEAM COMPETITION
Picture Dictionary Pages 140–146

ACTIVITY MASTERS
141 & 142

THE ACTIVITY

Teams compete to identify the sport being described.

GETTING READY

Students will do this activity in teams. Make a copy of Activity Master 141 (*Guess-the-Sport Cards 1*) and Activity Master 142 (*Guess-the-Sport Cards 2*). Cut the Activity Masters into separate cards. You will also need a watch with a second hand or a timer for this activity.

- **1.** Divide the class into two teams.

- **2.** Place *Guess-the-Sport Cards 1* in a pile face down for Team 1 to use and *Guess-the-Sport Cards 2* in a pile face down for Team 2 to use.

- **3.** Students from each team take turns picking a card from their team's pile. They must attempt to answer it in 10 seconds. If the answer is correct, their team earns a point. If not, a member of the other team has a chance to respond to that team's question before choosing his or her own card. If neither team answers successfully, the card goes to the bottom of the pile

    The team with the most points is the winner of the game.

WHAT ARE YOUR FAVORITE TYPES OF ENTERTAINMENT? *
CLASSROOM SEARCH
Picture Dictionary Pages 147–149

THE ACTIVITY

Students walk around the classroom asking each other about the types of music, plays, movies, and TV programs they like.

GETTING READY

Students will do this activity as a class. Make a copy of Activity Master 143 (*What Are Your Favorite Types of Entertainment?*) for each student in the class.

> **1.** Give a copy of *What Are Your Favorite Types of Entertainment?* to each student. Ask them to think about their favorite types of music, plays, movies, and TV programs.
>
> **2.** Write the following on the board for student reference during the activity:
>
>
>
> Do you like _____?
>
> **3.** Have students walk around asking each other the question on the board. When students have found someone who likes one of the types of entertainment on their grids, the responding student should write his or her name in that square of the grid (only one signature is necessary for each square).
>
> The student whose grid is filled with the most signatures is the winner of the game.

MUSIC & ENTERTAINMENT BOARD GAME **
BOARD GAME
Picture Dictionary Pages 147–150

THE ACTIVITY

Students play a board game that focuses on recreation and individual sports.

GETTING READY

Students will do this activity in groups. Make a copy of Activity Master 144 (*Music & Entertainment Board Game*) for each group.

Each group will need a die. You can duplicate Activity Master 7 (*Game Cube*) to make a die for each group, or students can use a coin. Each player will also need a marker (a button or anything small) and a piece of paper.

---

1. Divide the class into small groups.

2. Give a copy of the *Music & Entertainment Board Game* to each group. Also provide each group with a die, markers, and a piece of paper. If students use a coin as a die, the class should decide which side of the coin will indicate a move of one space and which will indicate a move of two spaces.

3. Have students place their markers on *Start*. The group should decide who goes first. That student begins the game by rolling the cube (or flipping the coin) and moving his or her marker. If the student responds to the question or task correctly, he or she may take one more turn. (The group decides if the response is correct.) If the student doesn't respond correctly, the next student takes a turn. No one may take more than two turns at a time.

Option 1: The first person to reach *Finish* is the winner.

Option 2: The game continues until each student reaches *Finish*. This way everybody is a winner.

 **16.1** WHAT'S DIFFERENT ABOUT THESE ZOOS? *
PICTURE DIFFERENCES
Picture Dictionary Pages 152–153

PAIRS

ACTIVITY MASTERS
145 & 146

THE ACTIVITY

Students work together to find differences between two zoos.

GETTING READY

Students will do this activity in pairs. Make copies of Activity Master 145 (*The East Coast Zoo*) for half the class and Activity Master 146 (*The West Coast Zoo*) for the other half of the class.

- **1.** Divide the class into pairs.

- **2.** Give a copy of *The East Coast Zoo* to one member of each pair and a copy of *The West Coast Zoo* to the other.

- **3.** Tell students that the object of the game is to find nine differences between the two zoos. Do one example before beginning the game. For example:

  The East Coast Zoo has a camel.
  The West Coast Zoo has a llama.

- **4.** When the activity is completed, call on students to tell the differences they found between the two zoos.

ANSWER KEY

The East Coast Zoo has . . .	The West Coast Zoo has . . .
a camel	a llama
a rhinoceros	a hippopotamus
a zebra	a horse
a giraffe	an elephant
a tiger	a lion
a polar bear	a moose
a gorilla	a chimpanzee
a fox	a wolf
a panda bear	a koala bear

NATURE FACT MEMORY CHALLENGE **

MEMORY GAME

Picture Dictionary Pages 154–155

ACTIVITY MASTERS
147 & 148

THE ACTIVITY

Students read information about birds, insects, fish, sea animals, and reptiles and try to remember it.

GETTING READY

Students will do this activity in pairs. Make copies of Activity Master 147 (*Interesting Nature Facts*) and Activity Master 148 (*Nature Fact Memory Challenge*) for each pair.

● **1.** Divide the class into pairs.

● **2.** Give each pair a copy of *Interesting Nature Facts*.

● **3.** Tell students that they will have 5 minutes to study the information carefully. After they have studied the information, tell them to put the Activity Master aside.

● **4.** Next give each pair a copy of *Nature Fact Memory Challenge*. Have them work together to complete Activity Master 148 based on their memory of the information on Activity Master 147.

● **5.** When students have completed the statements, have them look at Activity Master 147 again to check their answers.

ANSWER KEY

1. ostrich
2. mosquito
3. dolphin
4. whale
5. parrot
6. jellyfish
7. scorpion
8. turtle
9. owl
10. otter
11. peacock
12. alligator
13. hummingbird
14. robin
15. grasshopper
16. eagle

16.3

NAME THAT ANIMAL! **/***
TEAM COMPETITION
Picture Dictionary Pages 152–155

ACTIVITY MASTERS
149 & 150

THE ACTIVITY

Teams compete to answer questions about animals, birds, insects, fish, sea animals, and reptiles.

GETTING READY

Students will do this activity in teams. Make a copy of Activity Master 149 (*Animal Questions 1*) and Activity Master 150 (*Animal Questions 2*). Cut the Activity Masters into separate cards. You will also need a watch with a second hand or a timer for this activity.

1. Divide the class into two teams.

2. Place *Animal Questions 1* in a pile face down for Team 1 to use and *Animal Questions 2* in a pile face down for Team 2 to use.

3. Students from each team take turns picking a card from their team's pile. They must attempt to answer it in 10 seconds. If the answer is correct, their team earns a point. If not, a member of the other team has a chance to respond to that team's question before choosing his or her own card. If neither team answers successfully, the card goes to the bottom of the pile

    The team with the most points is the winner of the game.

16.4

GO TO THE FLORIST! *
PICK-A-CARD
Picture Dictionary Pages 156–157

PAIRS

ACTIVITY MASTER
151

THE ACTIVITY

Pairs of students attempt to get rid of all their cards by finding matches for cards in their hands.

GETTING READY

Students will do this activity in pairs. Make two copies of Activity Master 151 (*Tree, Plant, & Flower Cards*) for each pair. Cut each copy of Activity Master 151 into separate cards.

● **1.** Divide the class into pairs.

● **2.** Give each pair two sets of *Tree, Plant, and Flower Cards*.

● **3.** Write the following questions and answers on the board and have students practice saying them:

> A. Do you have a (*daisy*)?
> B. Yes, I do.
>
> A. Do you have an (*orchid*)?
> B. Sorry. I don't. Go to the florist!

● **4.** Have students shuffle the cards, take six cards each, and leave the remaining cards in a pile. The pair should then decide which player will go first.

● **5.** Each player looks at his or her cards and puts any matching pairs in a pile face up. Player A must now attempt to find the match for the cards remaining in his or her hand. To do so, the player asks: "Do you have a *daisy*?" If Player B has that card, he or she responds: "Yes, I do" and gives the card to Player A, who puts the matching cards in his or her pile. If Player B doesn't have the card, he or she tells Player A: "Sorry. I don't. Go to the florist!" In that case, Player A must *go to the florist* by picking a card from the pile. It is now Player B's turn to ask for a card.

The game continues until one player has no cards in his or her hand. The player with the most matching pairs wins the game.

16.5

WORLD-WIDE WEATHER ALERT! *

INFORMATION GAP

Picture Dictionary Page 159

PAIRS

**ACTIVITY MASTERS
152 & 153**

THE ACTIVITY

Students ask each other about missing weather alert information in different parts of the world.

GETTING READY

Students will do this activity in pairs. Make copies of Activity Master 152 (*World-Wide Weather Alert A*) for half the class and Activity Master 153 (*World-Wide Weather Alert B*) for the other half of the class.

● **1.** Divide the class into pairs.

● **2.** Give a copy of *World-Wide Weather Alert A* to one member of each pair and a copy of *World-Wide Weather Alert B* to the other.

● **3.** Tell students that each member of the pair knows different information about weather disasters taking place in different parts of the world. Have them ask each other questions to find the missing information and then write it in the appropriate place in their chart. For example:

    A. What's happening in Los Angeles?
    B. There's a wildfire in Los Angeles.

● **4.** When the pairs have completed the activity, have them compare their weather charts.

ENVIRONMENT & NATURE BOARD GAME **

BOARD GAME

Picture Dictionary Pages 156–159

THE ACTIVITY

Students play a board game that focuses on trees, plants, and flowers; energy, conservation, and the environment; and natural disasters.

GETTING READY

Students will do this activity in groups. Make a copy of Activity Master 154 (*Environment & Nature Board Game*) for each group.

Each group will need a die. You can duplicate Activity Master 7 (*Game Cube*) to make a die for each group, or students can use a coin. Each player will also need a marker (a button or anything small) and a piece of paper.

● **1.** Divide the class into small groups.

● **2.** Give a copy of the *Environment & Nature Board Game* to each group. Also provide each group with a die, markers, and a piece of paper. If students use a coin as a die, the class should decide which side of the coin will indicate a move of one space and which will indicate a move of two spaces.

● **3.** Have students place their markers on *Start*. The group should decide who goes first. That student begins the game by rolling the cube (or flipping the coin) and moving his or her marker. If the student responds to the question or task correctly, he or she may take one more turn. (The group decides if the response is correct.) If the student doesn't respond correctly, the next student takes a turn. No one may take more than two turns at a time.

Option 1: The first person to reach *Finish* is the winner.

Option 2: The game continues until each student reaches *Finish*. This way everybody is a winner.

 **MAY I SEE YOUR PASSPORT & VISA? ***
PICK-A-CARD
Picture Dictionary Page 160

ACTIVITY MASTER
155

THE ACTIVITY

Pairs of students attempt to get rid of all their cards by finding matches for cards in their hands.

GETTING READY

Students will do this activity in pairs. Make two copies of Activity Master 155 (*Forms of Identification Cards*) for each pair. Cut each copy of Activity Master 155 into separate cards.

● **1.** Divide the class into pairs.

● **2.** Give each pair two sets of *Forms of Identification Cards*.

● **3.** Write the following questions and answers on the board and have students practice saying them:

> A. May I see your passport and visa?
> B. Yes. Here you are.
>
> A. May I see your student I.D. and driver's license?
> B. I'm sorry. I don't have them. Keep looking!

● **4.** Have students shuffle the cards, take six cards each, and leave the remaining cards in a pile. The pair should then decide which player will go first.

Note that there are *two* forms of identification depicted on each card. Players must find matching cards on which *both* forms of identification are depicted.

● **5.** Each player looks at his or her cards and puts any matching pairs in a pile face up. Player A must now attempt to find the match for the cards remaining in his or her hand. To do so, the player asks: "May I see your passport and visa?" If Player B has the card with both of those forms of identification, he or she responds: "Yes. Here you are" and gives the card to Player A, who puts the matching cards in his or her pile. If Player B doesn't have the card, he or she tells Player A: "I'm sorry. I don't have them. Keep looking!" In that case, Player A must *keep looking* by picking a card from the pile. It is now Player B's turn to ask for a card.

The game continues until one player has no cards in his or her hand. The player with the most matching pairs wins the game.

17.2A U.S. GOVERNMENT BOARD GAME **

BOARD GAME

Picture Dictionary Page 161

THE ACTIVITY

Students play a board game that focuses on the structure of the U.S. government.

GETTING READY

Students will do this activity in groups. Make a copy of Activity Master 156 (*U.S. Government Board Game*) for each group.

Each group will need a die. You can duplicate Activity Master 7 (*Game Cube*) to make a die for each group, or students can use a coin. Each player will also need a marker (a button or anything small).

---

1. Divide the class into small groups.

2. Give a copy of the *U.S. Government Board Game* to each group. Also provide each group with a die and markers. If students use a coin as a die, the class should decide which side of the coin will indicate a move of one space and which will indicate a move of two spaces.

3. Have students place their markers on *Start*. The group should decide who goes first. That student begins the game by rolling the cube (or flipping the coin) and moving his or her marker. If the student responds to the question or task correctly, he or she may take one more turn. (The group decides if the response is correct.) If the student doesn't respond correctly, the next student takes a turn. No one may take more than two turns at a time.

Option 1: The first person to reach *Finish* is the winner.

Option 2: The game continues until each student reaches *Finish*. This way everybody is a winner.

17.3A

U.S. CIVICS QUESTION GAME **/***
TEAM COMPETITION
Picture Dictionary Pages 162–164

ACTIVITY MASTERS
157 & 158

THE ACTIVITY

Teams compete to answer questions about the U.S. Constitution, events in United States history, and U.S. holidays.

GETTING READY

Students will do this activity in teams. Make a copy of Activity Master 157 (*U.S. Civics Questions 1*) and Activity Master 158 (*U.S. Civics Questions 2*). Cut the Activity Masters into separate cards. You will also need a watch with a second hand or a timer for this activity.

● **1.** Divide the class into two teams.

● **2.** Place *U.S. Civics Questions 1* in a pile face down for Team 1 to use and *U.S. Civics Questions 2* in a pile face down for Team 2 to use.

● **3.** Students from each team take turns picking a card from their team's pile. They must attempt to answer it in 10 seconds. If the answer is correct, their team earns a point. If not, a member of the other team has a chance to respond to that team's question before choosing his or her own card. If neither team answers successfully, the card goes to the bottom of the pile

The team with the most points is the winner of the game.

17.4A

EVAN WAS ARRESTED! **/*
TELL-A-STORY
Picture Dictionary Page 165

ACTIVITY MASTER
159

THE ACTIVITY

Groups arrange a set of pictures in any order they wish and write a story about it.

GETTING READY

Students will do this activity in groups. Make a copy of Activity Master 159 (*Evan Story Cards*) for each group. Cut each copy of Activity Master 159 into separate cards.

- **1.** Divide the class into small groups.
- **2.** Give each group of set of *Evan Story Cards*.
- **3.** Have each group lay out the cards and decide what order to put them in. When they have decided the order they want, have them write a story about Evan's experience with the U.S. legal system.
- **4.** When everyone has finished, have the groups take turns telling the rest of the class their story about Evan's experience.

17.5A

MARIA MONTERO BECOMES
A CITIZEN **/***
TELL-A-STORY
Picture Dictionary Page 166

GROUPS

ACTIVITY MASTER
160

THE ACTIVITY

Groups arrange a set of pictures in any order they wish and write a story about it.

GETTING READY

Students will do this activity in groups. Make a copy of Activity Master 160 (*Maria Montero Story Cards*) for each group. Cut each copy of Activity Master 160 into separate cards.

- **1.** Divide the class into small groups.
- **2.** Give each group of set of *Maria Montero Story Cards*.
- **3.** Have each group lay out the cards and decide what order to put them in. When they have decided the order they want, have them write a story about Maria Montero's path to U.S. citizenship.
- **4.** When everyone has finished, have the groups take turns telling the rest of the class their story about how Maria Montero becomes a citizen.

17.6A

U.S. CIVICS BOARD GAME **
BOARD GAME
Picture Dictionary Pages 160–166

ACTIVITY MASTERS
7 & 161

THE ACTIVITY

Students play a board game that focuses on U.S. civics.

GETTING READY

Students will do this activity in groups. Make a copy of Activity Master 161 (*U.S. Civics Board Game*) for each group.

Each group will need a die. You can duplicate Activity Master 7 (*Game Cube*) to make a die for each group, or students can use a coin. Each player will also need a marker (a button or anything small).

● **1.** Divide the class into small groups.

● **2.** Give a copy of the *U.S. Civics Board Game* to each group. Also provide each group with a die and markers. If students use a coin as a die, the class should decide which side of the coin will indicate a move of one space and which will indicate a move of two spaces.

● **3.** Have students place their markers on *Start*. The group should decide who goes first. That student begins the game by rolling the cube (or flipping the coin) and moving his or her marker. If the student responds to the question or task correctly, he or she may take one more turn. (The group decides if the response is correct.) If the student doesn't respond correctly, the next student takes a turn. No one may take more than two turns at a time.

Option 1: The first person to reach *Finish* is the winner.

Option 2: The game continues until each student reaches *Finish*. This way everybody is a winner.

TRAVEL SEARCH GAME *
CLASSROOM SEARCH
Picture Dictionary Pages 160–162

THE ACTIVITY

Students walk around the classroom asking each other about travel experiences.

GETTING READY

Students will do this activity as a class. Make a copy of Activity Master 162 (*Did You Ever . . . ?*) for each student in the class.

- **1.** Give a copy of *Did You Ever . . . ?* to each student.

- **2.** Write the following on the board for student reference during the activity:

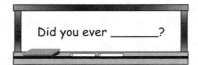

Did you ever _____?

- **3.** Have students walk around the room asking each other Yes/No questions about their travel experiences. For example, "Did you ever go on a cruise?" Students must answer truthfully. When students have found someone who did one of the activities on their grids, the responding student should write his or her name in that square of the grid (only one signature is necessary for each square). When Student A receives a positive response, that student should ask Student B the follow-up question (Where did you go?).

  The student whose grid is filled with the most signatures is the winner of the game. Have that student then report to the class about the information he or she learned.

INTERNATIONAL TRAVEL BOARD GAME **
BOARD GAME
Picture Dictionary Page 160–162

ACTIVITY MASTERS
7 & 163

THE ACTIVITY

Students play a board game that focuses on types of travel, arriving at a destination, and hotel communication.

GETTING READY

Students will do this activity in groups. Make a copy of Activity Master 163 (*International Travel Board Game*) for each group.

Each group will need a die. You can duplicate Activity Master 7 (*Game Cube*) to make a die for each group, or students can use a coin. Each player will also need a marker (a button or anything small).

- **1.** Divide the class into small groups.

- **2.** Give a copy of the *International Travel Board Game* to each group. Also provide each group with a die and markers. If students use a coin as a die, the class should decide which side of the coin will indicate a move of one space and which will indicate a move of two spaces.

- **3.** Have students place their markers on *Start*. The group should decide who goes first. That student begins the game by rolling the cube (or flipping the coin) and moving his or her marker. If the student responds to the question or task correctly, he or she may take one more turn. (The group decides if the response is correct.) If the student doesn't respond correctly, the next student takes a turn. No one may take more than two turns at a time.

   Option 1: The first person to reach *Finish* is the winner.

   Option 2: The game continues until each student reaches *Finish*. This way everybody is a winner.

17.3B

KENJI TOOK A TRIP **/***
TELL-A-STORY
Picture Dictionary Pages 161–163

GROUPS

ACTIVITY MASTER
164

THE ACTIVITY

Groups arrange a set of pictures in any order they wish and write a story about it.

GETTING READY

Students will do this activity in groups. Make a copy of Activity Master 164 (*Kenji Story Cards*) for each group. Cut each copy of Activity Master 164 into separate cards.

- **1.** Divide the class into small groups.
- **2.** Give each group of set of *Kenji Story Cards*.
- **3.** Have each group lay out the cards and decide what order to put them in. When they have decided the order they want, have them write a story about Kenji's trip.
- **4.** When everyone has finished, have the groups take turns telling the rest of the class their story about Kenji's experience.

17.4B MY TRIP **
LISTENING GAME
Picture Dictionary Page 163

PAIRS

ACTIVITY MASTERS
165 & 166

THE ACTIVITY

Students ask and answer questions in order to match what they did on their trips.

GETTING READY

Students will do this activity in pairs. Make a copy Activity Master 165 (*My Trip*) and Activity Master 166 (*Tourist Activity Cards*) for each student. Cut each copy of Activity Master 166 into separate cards.

● **1.** Divide the class into pairs.

● **2.** Give each student a copy of *My Trip* and a set of *Tourist Activity Cards*.

● **3.** Write the following on the board and have students use it as a model when doing the activity:

> A. Did you _____ on Monday?
> B. Yes, I did.
>   No, I didn't.

● **4.** Tell the class that all the Student As took a four-day trip to an exciting city. They should decide what city they visited. They should then think about what they did on each day of their trip and place two or more of the *Tourist Activity Cards* accordingly on those days.

● **5.** Student B must arrange the activities so that they match Student A's version by asking Yes/No questions about what Student A did on each day.

● **6.** When students have completed the activity, have them compare diagrams to make sure their activity cards are in the same days of the week.

● **7.** When each pair has completed the activity, have them reverse roles and play again. This time Student B takes a trip and Student A asks the questions.

17.5B

SOFIA'S VACATION **/***
TELL-A-STORY
Picture Dictionary Pages 163–165

**ACTIVITY MASTER
167**

THE ACTIVITY

Groups arrange a set of pictures in any order they wish and write a story about it.

GETTING READY

Students will do this activity in groups. Make a copy of Activity Master 167 (*Sofia Story Cards*) for each group. Cut each copy of Activity Master 167 into separate cards.

1. Divide the class into small groups.

2. Give each group of set of *Sofia Story Cards*. Tell the class that Sofia took a vacation last month. They should decide where she went and whether or not she enjoyed herself.

3. Have each group lay out the cards and decide what order to put them in. When they have decided the order they want, have them write a story about Sofia's vacation.

4. When everyone has finished, have the groups take turns telling the rest of the class their story about Sofia's experiences.

TOURIST BOARD GAME **
BOARD GAME
Picture Dictionary Pages 163–165

THE ACTIVITY

Students play a board game that focuses on tourist activities and tourist communication.

GETTING READY

Students will do this activity in groups. Make a copy of Activity Master 168 (*Tourist Board Game*) for each group.

Each group will need a die. You can duplicate Activity Master 7 (*Game Cube*) to make a die for each group, or students can use a coin. Each player will also need a marker (a button or anything small).

- **1.** Divide the class into small groups.

- **2.** Give a copy of the *Tourist Board Game* to each group. Also provide each group with a die and markers. If students use a coin as a die, the class should decide which side of the coin will indicate a move of one space and which will indicate a move of two spaces.

- **3.** Have students place their markers on *Start*. The group should decide who goes first. That student begins the game by rolling the cube (or flipping the coin) and moving his or her marker. If the student responds to the question or task correctly, he or she may take one more turn. (The group decides if the response is correct.) If the student doesn't respond correctly, the next student takes a turn. No one may take more than two turns at a time.

  Option 1: The first person to reach *Finish* is the winner.

  Option 2: The game continues until each student reaches *Finish*. This way everybody is a winner.

Activity Masters

Registration Form A   **1**

- Work with a partner. (Don't show this form to your partner.)
- Ask your partner about the missing information.
- Write the missing information.
- Read it back to your partner to check your answers.

Registration Form

NAME: _____ B. _____

ADDRESS: 35 Main Street   APT. _____

            Oakdale, CA 95361

TELEPHONE: _____   CELL PHONE: 209-555-7348

E-MAIL ADDRESS: _____   SSN: 227-98-8561

SEX: M ____   F ____

DATE OF BIRTH: 1/18/1967   PLACE OF BIRTH: _____

- Work with a partner. (Don't show this form to your partner.)
- Ask your partner about the missing information.
- Write the missing information.
- Read it back to your partner to check your answers.

Registration Form

NAME: Tracy _____ Lee

ADDRESS: _____ APT. 7B

Oakdale, CA 95361

TELEPHONE: 209-555-2673   CELL PHONE: _____

E-MAIL ADDRESS: tracy77@wbw.com   SSN: _____

SEX: M ____   F ____

DATE OF BIRTH: 1/18/1967   PLACE OF BIRTH: San Diego, CA

- Work with a partner. (Don't look at your partner's family tree.)
- Ask your partner questions to find out the names of family members that are missing from your family tree.
- Write the names under the appropriate person.
- Compare your family tree with your partner's.

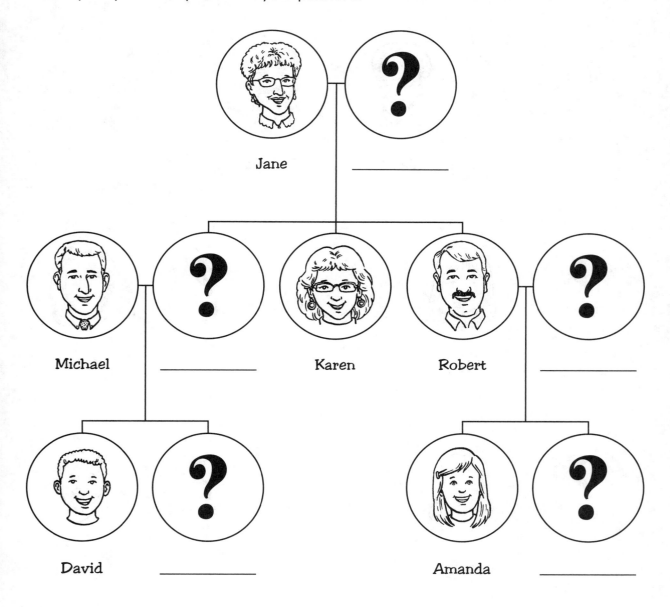

Jane

Michael   Karen   Robert

David   Amanda

- Work with a partner. (Don't look at your partner's family tree.)
- Ask your partner questions to find out the names of family members that are missing from your family tree.
- Write the names under the appropriate person.
- Compare your family tree with your partner's.

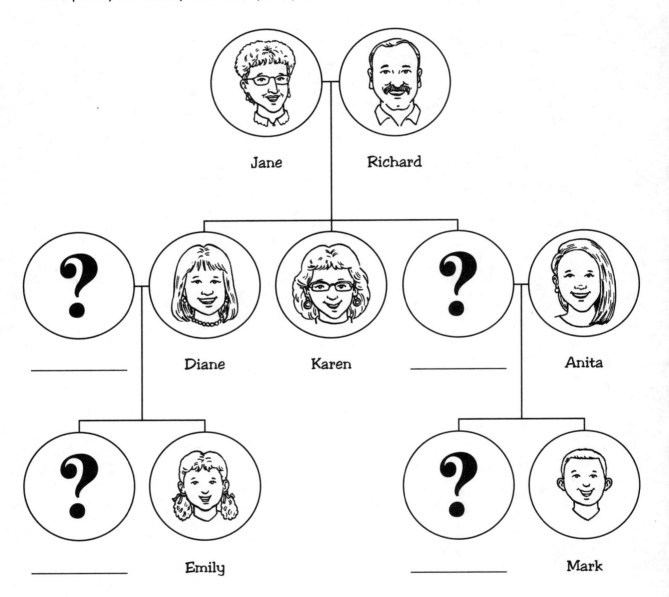

Jane   Richard

_____   Diane   Karen   _____   Anita

_____   Emily   _____   Mark

- Put your markers on *Start*.
- Take turns tossing the Game Cube (or flipping a coin) to move your marker around the board.
- Follow the instructions in each space.

START

Say and write your first name, middle initial, and last name.

What's your place of birth?

What's your city and state?

Pick a Family Member Card!
_____
Finish the sentence.

What's another word for "telephone number"?

How many numbers are in a zip code?

What are **2** other words for "last name"?

Finish the sentence:
"My mother and father are my _____."

Pick a Family Member Card!
_____
Finish the sentence.

How many numbers are in an area code and telephone number?

Finish the sentence:
"My brother and sister are my _____."

FINISH

Pick a Family Member Card!
_____
Finish the sentence.

How many numbers are in a social security number?

Family Member Cards

My son's wife is my . . .	My daughter's son is my . . .	My son's daughter is my . . .
My husband's brother is my . . .	My wife's sister is my . . .	My wife's father is my . . .
My husband's mother is my . . .	My daughter's husband is my . . .	My mother's father is my . . .
My father's mother is my . . .	My brother's son is my . . .	My sister's daughter is my . . .
My mother's brother is my . . .	My father's sister is my . . .	My uncle's son is my . . .

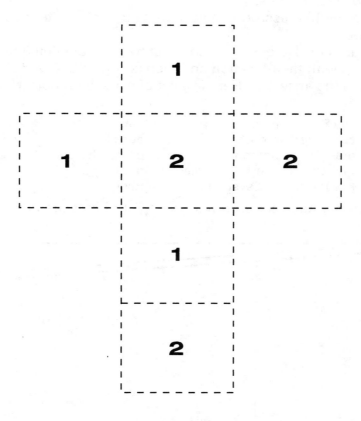

Copy and cut out this diagram to make a cube.
Fold along the lines and tape it together.

My Classroom

- Work with a partner. (Don't show this classroom to your partner.) You also each have a set of *Classroom Object Cards*.
- One of you chooses eight Classroom Object Cards and places them anywhere you wish in the classroom.
- The other person asks Yes/No questions in order to find out what items are in the classroom along with their location and then arranges the cards in his or her classroom based on the answers. Here is a list of classroom objects you can ask about:

book	clock	map	pen	screen
bookcase	computer	mouse	pencil	spiral notebook
bulletin board	eraser	notebook	pencil sharpener	wastebasket
calculator	globe	overhead projector	printer	
chalkboard	keyboard	P.A. system	ruler	

- Compare with your partner's classroom to see if your items are in the same places.

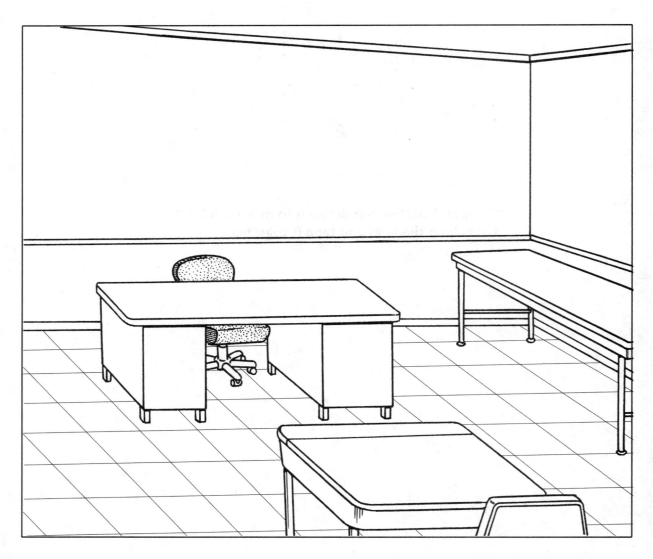

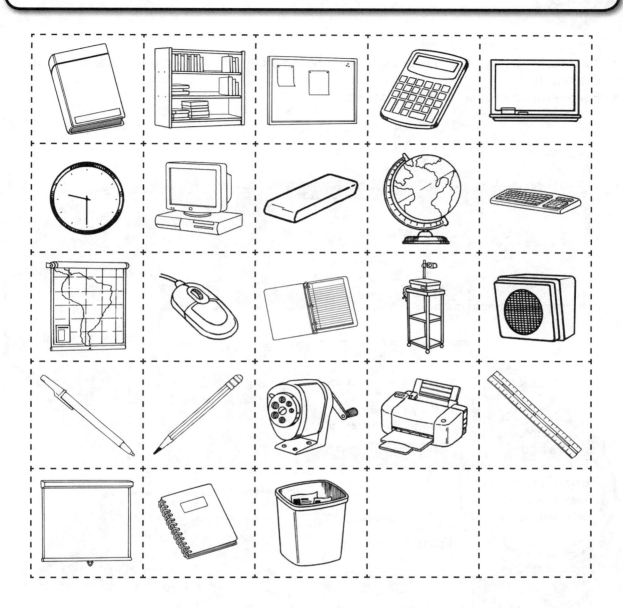

- Put your markers on *Start.*
- Take turns tossing the Game Cube (or flipping a coin) to move your marker around the board.
- Follow the instructions in each space.

START

Who are **2** people in a classroom?

What are **3** things on the wall of a classroom?

Name **3** "computer" items in a classroom.

Tell **3** things you write with in a classroom.

What are **3** things in the classroom that begin with the letter "p"?

Pick a Classroom Action Card!
___
Answer the question.

In 15 seconds . . . name 3 classroom items you have with you today.

Draw a classroom item.
Everyone has to guess what it is.

Tell the location of something in your classroom. Can your classmates guess what it is?

What are **3** things in the classroom that begin with the letter "m"?

FINISH

Look at the front of your classroom.
SING A SONG ABOUT WHAT YOU SEE!
♪ ♪

Pick a Classroom Action Card!
___
Answer the question.

Classroom Action Cards

11

I want to ask the teacher a question. What should I do?

Complete these classroom actions:

_____ your name.
_____ your name.
_____ your name.

Complete these classroom actions:

_____ your book.
_____ your book.
_____ your book.

Complete these classroom actions:

_____ the board.
_____ the board.

Tell 3 things pairs of students can do.

What are 3 "dictionary" actions?

What are 3 ways students can "work" in a classroom?

What's the action?

4. My _____ is Jones.
a. last name
b. zip code
c. address

What's the action?

I'm from Chicago 1985 phone number

What's the action?

The *map* is on the wall.

What's the action?

1. name — 129 Elm
2. city — Maria
3. addr — Los An

What's the action?

Help each other.

What's the action?

wife
sister
~~son~~
aunt
daughter

What's the action?

etdusnt
student

What's the action?

dictionary. in Look the

Look in the dictionary

2.2   *Classroom & Classroom Actions Board Game*
INFORMATION GAP
Word by Word Communication Games & Activity Masters, Page 5

© 2010 Pearson Education
Duplication for classroom use is permitted.

What Do You Do Every Day? 12

- Ask other students about their everyday activities.
- When you find someone whose activity is on your grid, have that person write his or her name in that square.
- The first student with the most signatures wins the game.

Take a Bath Every Day? Name _____	**Shave Every Day?** Name _____	**Make Dinner Every Day?** Name _____
Put on Makeup Every Day? Name _____	**Make the Bed Every Day?** Name _____	**Wash the Dishes Every Day?** Name _____
Walk the Dog Every Day? Name _____	**Take the Bus to Work or School Every Day?** Name _____	**Watch TV Every Day?** Name _____
Listen to the Radio Every Day? Name _____	**Read the Newspaper Every Day?** Name _____	**Play the Guitar Every Day?** Name _____
Exercise Every Day? Name _____	**Use the Computer Every Day?** Name _____	**Relax Every Day?** Name _____

- Work with a partner. Look at each other's pictures.
- There are eight differences between the Lopez family's activities and the Gomez family's activities.
- Talk with your partner about the differences and write them in the chart below.

The Lopez Family	The Gomez Family
1. The father is cleaning the house.	**1.** The father is doing the laundry.
2. The mother	**2.** The mother
3. The older son	**3.** The older son
4. The younger son	**4.** The younger son
5. The older daughter	**5.** The older daughter
6. The younger daughter	**6.** The younger daughter
7. The grandmother	**7.** The grandmother
8. The grandfather	**8.** The grandfather

- Work with a partner. Look at each other's pictures.
- There are eight differences between the Lopez family's activities and the Gomez family's activities.
- Talk with your partner about the differences and write them in the chart below.

The Lopez Family	**The Gomez Family**
1. The father is cleaning the house.	**1.** The father is doing the laundry.
2. The mother	**2.** The mother
3. The older son	3. The older son
4. The younger son	**4.** The younger son
5. The older daughter	**5.** The older daughter
6. The younger daughter	**6.** The younger daughter
7. The grandmother	**7.** The grandmother
8. The grandfather	**8.** The grandfather

Alan's Daily Routine

- Work with your partner. (Don't look at each other's schedules.)
- You have information about Alan's Daily Routine. Your partner has information about Ellen.
- Ask your partner about the things Ellen does every day before and after work. Write the activities in the chart below.
- Compare schedules with your partner after you complete the activity.

Alan's Daily Routine

Before work:	*After work:*
shave	make dinner
comb his hair	feed the baby
eat breakfast	walk the dog
feed the cat	watch TV
go to work	use the computer

Ellen's Daily Routine

Before work:	After work:
She takes a shower.	

Ellen's Daily Routine 16

- Work with your partner. (Don't look at each other's schedules.)
- You have information about Ellen's Daily Routine. Your partner has information about Alan.
- Ask your partner about the things Alan does every day before and after work. Write the activities in the chart below.
- Compare schedules with your partner after you complete the activity.

Ellen's Daily Routine

Before work:	*After work:*
take a shower	go to the store
brush my teeth	eat dinner
make the bed	wash the dishes
make breakfast	read a book
feed the baby	relax

Alan's Daily Routine

Before work:	**After work:**
He shaves.	

- Put your markers on *Start.*
- Take turns tossing the Game Cube (or flipping a coin) to move your marker around the board.
- Follow the instructions in each space.

START

What are **3** things you do every morning?

What are **3** things you do every evening?

What are **3** things people "play"?

What are **3** household "chores"?

What are **3** things you do to get ready to go to work or school?

Pick a Pantomime Card!
PANTOMIME THE ACTION.
Everyone has to guess what you're doing.

What are **3** things you do every day that you like?

In 15 seconds...
Put in order:
take a shower
get dressed
go to school
get up

Pick a Pantomime Card!
PANTOMIME THE ACTION.
Everyone has to guess what you're doing.

In 15 seconds...
Put in order:
sleep
come home
go to work
go to bed

FINISH

What are **3** things you do on your day off?
SING A SONG ABOUT THEM! ♪ ♫

What are **3** things you do every day that you *don't like?*

brush my teeth	drive to work	exercise	feed the cat
get dressed	make the bed	plant flowers	play basketball
play cards	play the guitar	put on makeup	read the newspaper
relax	shave	swim	take a bath
take a shower	walk the dog	wash the dishes	write a letter

Everyday Conversation Cards

19

A	B	A	B
What's new?	Not much.	How are you?	Fine, thanks.
Good-bye.	See you later.	Hello. My name is Pat.	Nice to meet you.
Thank you.	You're welcome.	How are you doing?	Okay.
Nice to meet you.	Nice to meet you, too.	May I please speak to Maria?	Maria? Yes. Hold on a moment.
May I please speak to Mr. Lee?	I'm sorry. He isn't here right now.	Good morning.	Good morning.
Good afternoon.	Good afternoon.	Good evening.	Good evening.

2.7 *What's New? Not Much.*
PICK-A-CARD
Word by Word Communication Games & Activity Masters, Page 10

© 2010 Pearson Education
Duplication for classroom use is permitted.

Everyday Conversation Board Game

20

- Put your markers on *Start.*
- Take turns tossing the Game Cube (or flipping a coin) to move your marker around the board.
- Follow the instructions in each space.

START

You see a friend. Greet your friend!

Someone says "Good-bye." What are **3** ways to respond?

What are **2** ways to respond to "What's new?"

Introduce yourself to your classmates!

What do you say to get someone's attention?

What are **2** ways to respond to "How are you doing?"

Someone says, "Thanks." What do you say?

What are **2** ways to ask someone to repeat something?

Someone says, "Nice to meet you." What do you say?

What are **2** ways to say you don't understand something?

What are **3** ways to respond to "How are you?"

You want to speak to someone on the phone. What do you say?

FINISH

Introduce one classmate to another.

World-Wide Weather A

21

- Work with a partner. (Don't show your chart to your partner.)
- You know the weather and temperatures in some cities around the world. Your partner knows the weather and temperature in other cities. Ask your partner about the information that's missing from your chart. Complete the chart with the information you learn from your partner.
- Compare your answers after you complete your charts.

 sunny

 clear

 smoggy

 raining

 snowing

 hailing

 cloudy

 foggy

 windy

 drizzling

 lightning

 thunderstorms

City	Weather	Temp
Beijing		
Cairo		90°F
London		
Los Angeles		83°F
Mexico City		
New York		45°F

City	Weather	Temp
Paris		53°F
San Juan		
São Paulo		77°F
Seoul		
Tokyo		39°F
Toronto		

- Work with a partner. (Don't show your chart to your partner.)
- You know the weather and temperatures in some cities around the world. Your partner knows the weather and temperature in other cities. Ask your partner about the information that's missing from your chart. Complete the chart with the information you learn from your partner.
- Compare your answers after you complete your charts.

sunny

clear

smoggy

raining

snowing

hailing

cloudy

foggy

windy

drizzling

lightning

thunderstorms

City	Weather	Temp
Beijing		30°F
Cairo		
London		55°F
Los Angeles		
Mexico City		77°F
New York		

City	Weather	Temp
Paris		
San Juan		82°F
São Paulo		
Seoul		40°F
Tokyo		
Toronto		28°F

- Ask other students about time, money, and dates on the calendar.
- When you find someone who answers "yes" to a question on your grid, have that person write his or her name in that square.
- The first student with the most signatures wins the game.

Get Up at 5:30? Name _____	**Go to School or Work at 8:00?** Name _____	**Eat Dinner at 6:00?** Name _____
Go to Bed at 10:30? Name _____	**Have Three Quarters in Your Pocket or Purse?** Name _____	**Have a Five-Dollar Bill in Your Pocket or Purse?** Name _____
Have a Twenty-Dollar Bill in Your Pocket or Purse? Name _____	**Have a Birthday in January?** Name _____	**Have a Birthday in July?** Name _____
Have an Anniversary in March? Name _____	**Have an Anniversary in November?** Name _____	**Have an Appointment Next Week?** Name _____
Exercise Every Day? Name _____	**Watch TV Every Day?** Name _____	**Go to the Store Twice a Week?** Name _____

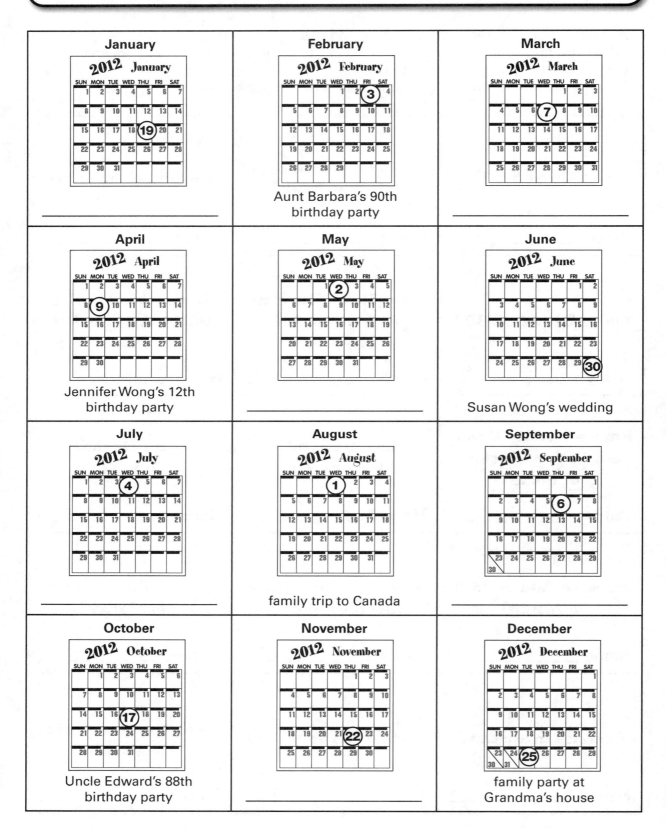

January

2012 January

SUN	MON	TUE	WED	THU	FRI	SAT
1	2	3	4	5	6	7
8	9	10	11	12	13	14
15	16	17	(19)	20	21	
22	23	24	25	26	27	28
29	30	31				

_____

February

2012 February

SUN	MON	TUE	WED	THU	FRI	SAT
			1	2	(3)	4
5	6	7	8	9	10	11
12	13	14	15	16	17	18
19	20	21	22	23	24	25
26	27	28	29			

Aunt Barbara's 90th birthday party

March

2012 March

SUN	MON	TUE	WED	THU	FRI	SAT
				1	2	3
4	5	6	(7)	8	9	10
11	12	13	14	15	16	17
18	19	20	21	22	23	24
25	26	27	28	29	30	31

_____

April

2012 April

SUN	MON	TUE	WED	THU	FRI	SAT
1	2	3	4	5	6	7
8	(9)	10	11	12	13	14
15	16	17	18	19	20	21
22	23	24	25	26	27	28
29	30					

Jennifer Wong's 12th birthday party

May

2012 May

SUN	MON	TUE	WED	THU	FRI	SAT
		1	(2)	3	4	5
6	7	8	9	10	11	12
13	14	15	16	17	18	19
20	21	22	23	24	25	26
27	28	29	30	31		

_____

June

2012 June

SUN	MON	TUE	WED	THU	FRI	SAT
					1	2
3	4	5	6	7	8	9
10	11	12	13	14	15	16
17	18	19	20	21	22	23
24	25	26	27	28	29	(30)

Susan Wong's wedding

July

2012 July

SUN	MON	TUE	WED	THU	FRI	SAT
1	2	3	(4)	5	6	7
8	9	10	11	12	13	14
15	16	17	18	19	20	21
22	23	24	25	26	27	28
29	30	31				

_____

August

2012 August

SUN	MON	TUE	WED	THU	FRI	SAT
			(1)	2	3	4
5	6	7	8	9	10	11
12	13	14	15	16	17	18
19	20	21	22	23	24	25
26	27	28	29	30	31	

family trip to Canada

September

2012 September

SUN	MON	TUE	WED	THU	FRI	SAT
						1
2	3	4	5	(6)	7	8
9	10	11	12	13	14	15
16	17	18	19	20	21	22
23/30	24	25	26	27	28	29

_____

October

2012 October

SUN	MON	TUE	WED	THU	FRI	SAT
	1	2	3	4	5	6
7	8	9	10	11	12	13
14	15	16	(17)	18	19	20
21	22	23	24	25	26	27
28	29	30	31			

Uncle Edward's 88th birthday party

November

2012 November

SUN	MON	TUE	WED	THU	FRI	SAT
				1	2	3
4	5	6	7	8	9	10
11	12	13	14	15	16	17
18	19	20	21	(22)	23	24
25	26	27	28	29	30	

_____

December

2012 December

SUN	MON	TUE	WED	THU	FRI	SAT
						1
2	3	4	5	6	7	8
9	10	11	12	13	14	15
16	17	18	19	20	21	22
23/30	24/31	(25)	26	27	28	29

family party at Grandma's house

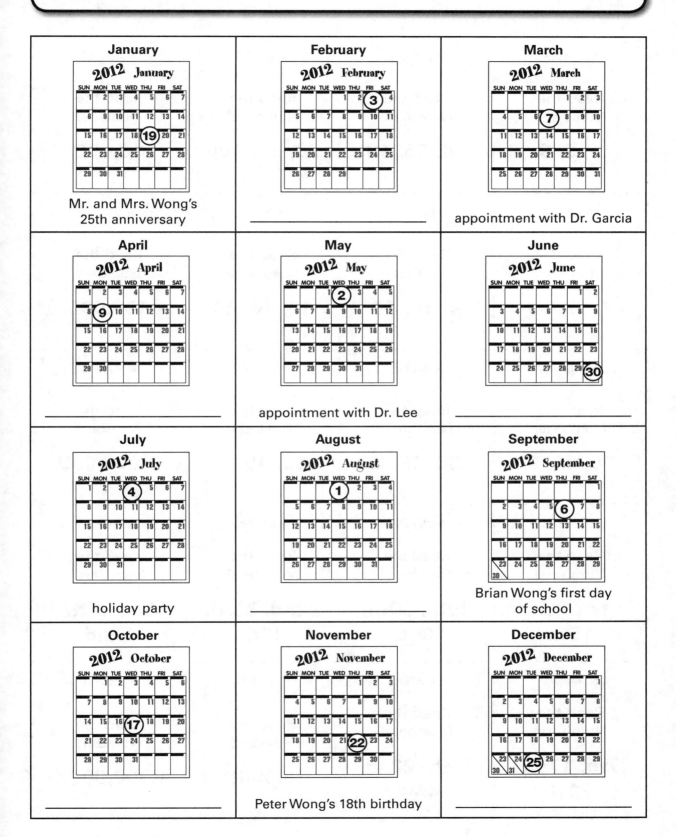

January	February	March
2012 January	2012 February	2012 March
Mr. and Mrs. Wong's 25th anniversary (19)	(3)	appointment with Dr. Garcia (7)

April	May	June
2012 April	2012 May	2012 June
(9)	appointment with Dr. Lee (2)	(30)

July	August	September
2012 July	2012 August	2012 September
holiday party (4)	(1)	Brian Wong's first day of school (6)

October	November	December
2012 October	2012 November	2012 December
(17)	Peter Wong's 18th birthday (22)	(25)

Number Questions

NUMBERS	NUMBERS	NUMBERS	NUMBERS
Read the Numbers! **1, 5, 8**	Read the Numbers! **14, 16, 18**	Read the Numbers! **30, 70, 100**	Read the Number! **10,000**
Read the Numbers! **7, 17, 70**	Read the Numbers! **4, 14, 40**	Read the Numbers! **16, 16, 60**	Read the Number! **100,000**
Read the Numbers! **90, 19, 9**	Read the Numbers! **80, 18, 8**	Read the Numbers! **50, 15, 5**	Read the Number! **1,000,000**
Read the Numbers! **1st, 9th, 15th**	Read the Numbers! **20th, 50th, 100th**	Read the Numbers! **22nd, 33rd, 48th**	Read the Numbers! **6th, 16th, 62nd**
Read the Numbers! **7th, 17th, 71st**	Read the Numbers! **11th, 22nd, 44th**	Read the Number! **10,000th**	Read the Number! **1,000,000th**

Time Questions

27

TIME	TIME	TIME	TIME
What time is it?	What time is it?	What time is it?	What time is it?
TIME	TIME	TIME	TIME
What time is it?	What time is it?	What time is it?	What time is it?
TIME	TIME	TIME	TIME
What time is it?	What time is it?	What time is it?	What time is it?
TIME	TIME	TIME	TIME
What time is it?	What time is it?	What time is it?	What time is it?
TIME	TIME	TIME	TIME
What time is it?	What time is it?	What time is it?	What time is it?

3.3 *Number-Time-Money-Calendar Game*
TEAM COMPETITION
Word by Word Communication Games & Activity Masters, Page 15

© 2010 Pearson Education
Duplication for classroom use is permitted.

MONEY	MONEY	MONEY	MONEY
How much is three quarters?	How much is two dimes, one quarter, and three nickels?	How much is three pennies, two quarters, and a half dollar?	How much is ten dimes, two nickels, and three quarters?
MONEY	MONEY	MONEY	MONEY
How much is a silver dollar, six dimes, and two quarters?	How much is six quarters, two dimes, a nickel, and a ten-dollar bill?	How much is three silver dollars, four dimes, a penny, and two twenty-dollar bills?	How much is seven nickels, twelve pennies, a five-dollar bill, and a ten-dollar bill?
MONEY	MONEY	MONEY	MONEY
How much is a penny, two nickels, six quarters, and a five-dollar bill?	How much is eight quarters, ten dimes, and two half dollars?	How much is a quarter, a half dollar, a silver dollar, and two fifty-dollar bills?	What's the amount? **$56.49**
MONEY	MONEY	MONEY	MONEY
What's the amount? **$128.63**	What's the amount? **$84.22**	What's the amount? **$79.10**	What's the amount? **$100.45**
MONEY	MONEY	MONEY	MONEY
What's the amount? **$10.50**	What's the amount? **$1.30**	What's the amount? **$61.80**	What's the amount? **$31.97**

Calendar Questions

29

CALENDAR **What month comes before December?**	CALENDAR **What month comes after September?**	CALENDAR **What month comes before August?**	CALENDAR **What month comes after February?**
CALENDAR **What day comes before Wednesday?**	CALENDAR **What day comes after Saturday?**	CALENDAR **What day comes before Friday?**	CALENDAR **What day comes between Tuesday and Thursday?**
CALENDAR **Name two spring months.**	CALENDAR **Name two summer months.**	CALENDAR **Name two fall months.**	CALENDAR **Name two winter months.**
CALENDAR **What are the first six months of the year?**	CALENDAR **What are the last six months of the year?**	CALENDAR **When is your birthday?**	CALENDAR **What's today's date?**
CALENDAR **Name something you do once a week.**	CALENDAR **Name something you do every day.**	CALENDAR **Tell something you did last week.**	CALENDAR **Tell something you're going to do next week.**

- Work with a partner. Look at each other's living rooms.
- There are ten differences between Bruno's living room and Brenda's living room.
- Talk with your partner about the differences and write them in the chart below.

In Bruno's Living Room	**In Brenda's Living Room**
1. There's one floor lamp.	1. There are two floor lamps.
2.	2.
3.	3.
4.	4.
5.	5.
6.	6.
7.	7.
8.	8.
9.	9.
10.	10.

- Work with a partner. Look at each other's living rooms.
- There are ten differences between Bruno's living room and Brenda's living room.
- Talk with your partner about the differences and write them in the chart below.

In Bruno's Living Room	In Brenda's Living Room
1. There's one floor lamp.	1. There are two floor lamps.
2.	2.
3.	3.
4.	4.
5.	5.
6.	6.
7.	7.
8.	8.
9.	9.
10.	10.

- Put your markers on *Start.*
- Take turns tossing the Game Cube (or flipping a coin) to move your marker around the board.
- Follow the instructions in each space.

START

What are **5** things 🎵 you have in your living room? 🎵 Sing a song about them!

What are **3** things you find in a baby's room?

In 20 seconds . . . name **3** different types of housing.

Pick a Home Object card! **Draw the item.** Everyone has to guess what it is.

What are **5** things 🎵 you have in your bedroom? 🎵 Sing a song about them!

In 20 seconds . . . name **3** things in the front of a home.

In 20 seconds . . . name **3** things in the backyard of a home.

What are **5** things 🎵 you have in your kitchen? 🎵 Sing a song about them!

Pick a Home Object card! **Draw the item.** Everyone has to guess what it is.

What are **5** things 🎵 you have in your bathroom? 🎵 Sing a song about them!

In 20 seconds . . . name **5** things in a place setting.

FINISH

What's your favorite room at home? Tell why.

Home Object Cards

35

baby carriage	bed	candlestick	chandelier
crib	cup and saucer	floor lamp	high chair
knife, fork, and spoon	lamp	mirror	pillow
plant	rattle	refrigerator	salt shaker
teddy bear	toaster	TV	vase

4.3   *At Home Board Game*
BOARD GAME
Word by Word Communication Games & Activity Masters, Page 18

© 2010 Pearson Education
Duplication for classroom use is permitted.

- Work with a partner. You're looking for an apartment. Your partner is the realtor.
- Ask the following questions about the building on Maple Street and write the answers.
- Compare your answers with your partner's information about the apartment.

1. How long is the lease for?   _____

2. How much is the security deposit?   _____

3. How many floors are there in the building?   _____

4. How many apartments are there in the building?   _____

5. Is there a doorman in the building?   _____

6. Is there a superintendent?   _____

7. Is there a fire escape and fire exit?   _____

8. Is there parking for tenants and guests?   _____

9. Is there an elevator in the building?   _____

10. Where are the mailboxes?   _____

11. Is there a storage room?   _____

12. Is there a laundry room?   _____

13. How many rooms are there in the apartment?   _____

14. How many bedrooms are there?   _____

15. Is there a refrigerator in the kitchen?   _____

16. Is there an air conditioner?   _____

17. Is there a balcony?   _____

18. Is there a smoke detector?   _____

19. Is there a dead-bolt lock?   _____

- Work with a partner. Your partner is looking for an apartment. You're the realtor.
- Answer your partner's questions about the building on Maple Street.
- Compare your partner's answers with the information you have.

123 Maple Street
Apt. 2A

Lease

12 month lease
$800.00 security deposit

About the Building

4 floors
16 apartments in the building
doorman 6:00 A.M. to 9:00 P.M.
superintendent lives in basement apartment
fire escape
fire exit
parking garage for tenants
parking lot for guests
no elevator
mailboxes on the first floor
storage room in the basement
no laundry room

About the Apartment

four rooms
one bedroom
stove in kitchen, no refrigerator
air conditioner
no balcony
smoke detector
dead-bolt lock

- Work with a partner. Look at each other's houses.
- There are eight differences between problems in the Wilsons' House and the Watsons' house.
- Talk with your partner about the differences and write them in the chart below.

In the Wilsons' House	In the Watsons' House
1. The bathtub is leaking.	**1.** The sink is leaking.
2.	**2.**
3.	**3.**
4.	**4.**
5.	**5.**
6.	**6.**
7.	**7.**
8.	**8.**

4.5   *What's Different About These Houses?*
PICURE DIFFERENCES
Word by Word Communication Games & Activity Masters, Page 20

© 2010 Pearson Education
Duplication for classroom use is permitted.

- Work with a partner. Look at each other's houses.
- There are eight differences between problems in the Wilsons' House and the Watsons' house.
- Talk with your partner about the differences and write them in the chart below.

In the Wilsons' House	In the Watsons' House
1. The bathtub is leaking.	**1.** The sink is leaking.
2.	**2.**
3.	**3.**
4.	**4.**
5.	**5.**
6.	**6.**
7.	**7.**
8.	**8.**

Household Item Word Clue Cards

Name That Cleaning Item!

1. It's liquid.
2. You spray it.
3. You use it to wash windows.

WINDOW CLEANER

Name That Cleaning Item!

1. It's liquid.
2. You use a mop with it.
3. You use it to clean the floor.

FLOOR WAX

Name That Cleaning Item!

1. It has a long handle.
2. You use it on the floor.
3. You use it to sweep the floor.

BROOM

Name That Cleaning Item!

1. They're round.
2. You use them to dry things.
3. They're paper.

PAPER TOWELS

Name That Cleaning Item!

1. It's noisy.
2. You sometimes use attachments.
3. You use it to clean the carpet.

VACUUM

Name That Cleaning Item!

1. It has a short handle.
2. You use it to dust.
3. It has feathers.

FEATHER DUSTER

Name That Home Supply!

1. You use it in the bathroom.
2. It has a long handle.
3. You use it to fix the toilet.

PLUNGER

Name That Home Supply!

1. It's long.
2. It's metal.
3. It has inches and feet.

MEASURING TAPE

Name That Tool!

1. It's electric.
2. It's noisy.
3. You use it to cut wood.

ELECTRIC SAW

Name That Tool!

1. It has a round handle.
2. It's long.
3. You use it with screws.

SCREWDRIVER

Name That Tool!

1. It has two handles.
2. It opens and closes.
3. You use it to hold small things.

PLIERS

Name That Gardening Tool!

1. It's long.
2. There's water in it.
3. You use it to water the flowers.

GARDEN HOSE

- Work with a partner. (Don't show this map to your partner.)
- Ask your partner about the buildings that aren't on your map.
- Write the names on the buildings.
- Compare maps with your partner.

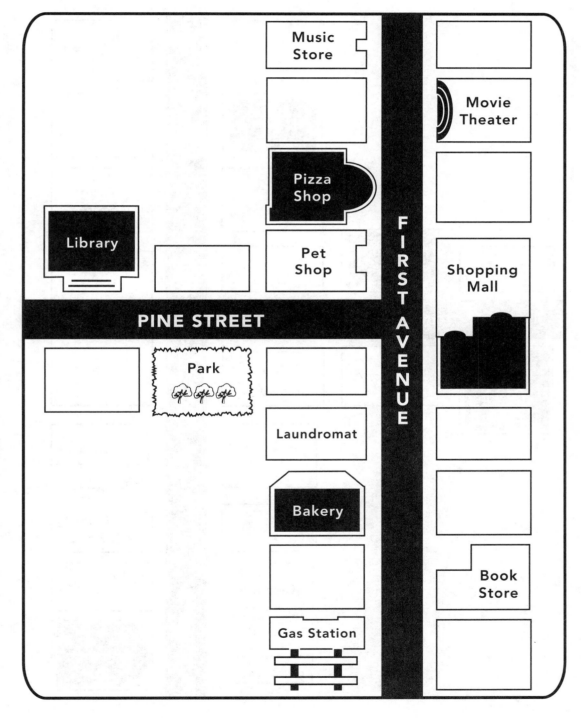

- Work with a partner. (Don't show this map to your partner.)
- Ask your partner about the buildings that aren't on your map.
- Write the names on the buildings.
- Compare maps with your partner.

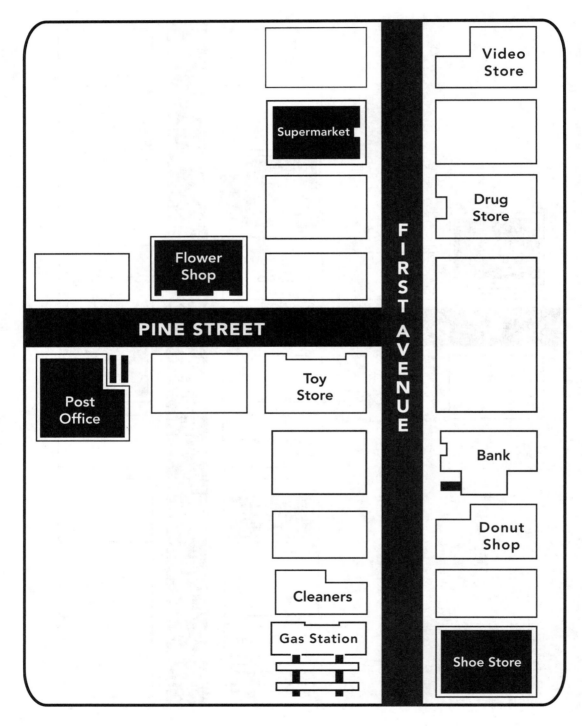

Places Around Town Cards

5.3   *What's the Place?*
LISTENING GRID
Word by Word Communication Games & Activity Masters, Page 24

- Work with a partner. (Don't show your map to your partner.)
- One of you places the build-a-city cards on your own map and tells the other person where to put them on his or her map.
- Compare maps with your partner.

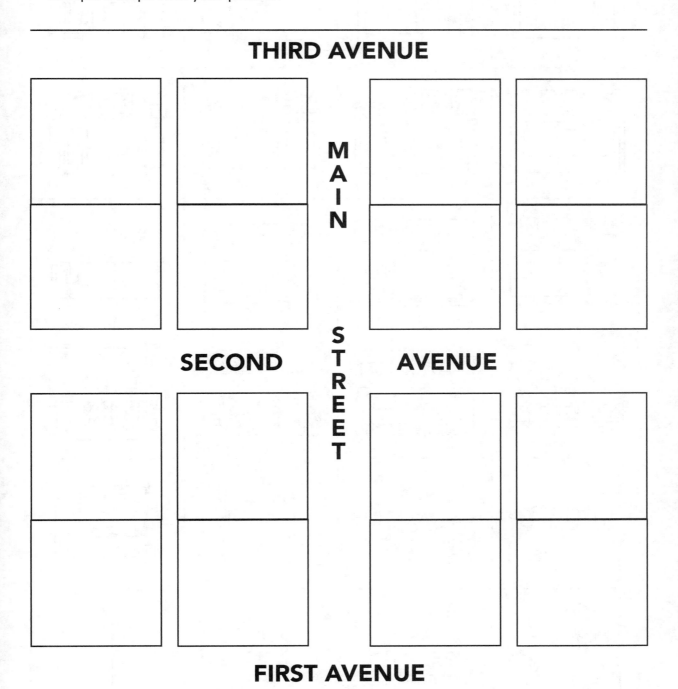

THIRD AVENUE

M A I N

SECOND

S T R E E T

AVENUE

FIRST AVENUE

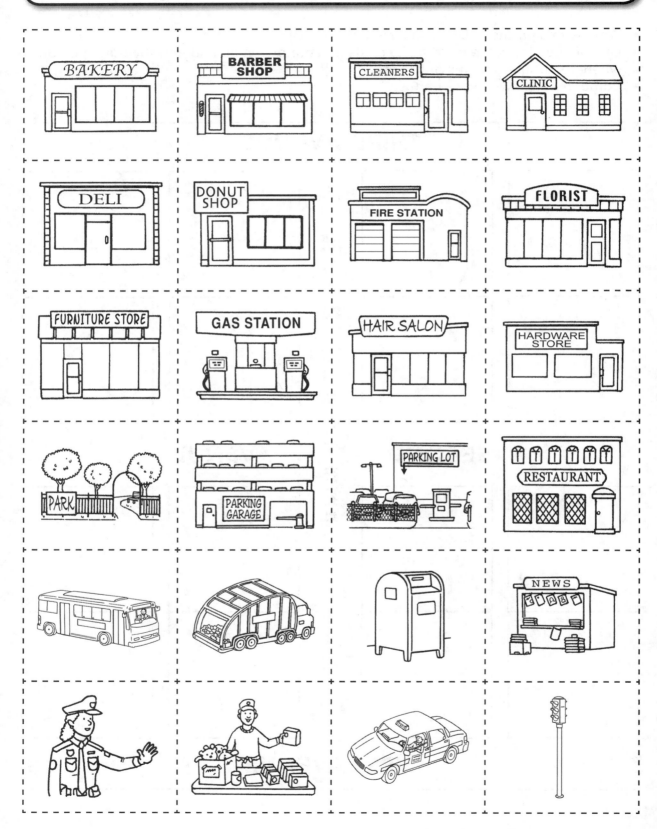

Name That Place!

1. It's noisy.
2. People go there to travel to another place.
3. Tickets are cheaper than plane or train tickets.

BUS STATION

Name That Place!

1. There are a lot of movies there.
2. You need to have a membership card.
3. You can rent DVDs to watch at home.

VIDEO STORE

Name That Place!

1. You can buy a lot of different things there.
2. You go there to save money.
3. You go there to pay very low prices.

DISCOUNT STORE

Name That Place!

1. You go there to buy tickets.
2. You go there to plan a vacation.
3. You meet with a travel agent there.

TRAVEL AGENCY

Name That Place!

1. People go there with shirts and pants.
2. People go there with their dirty clothing.
3. This place has washing machines.

LAUNDROMAT

Name That Place!

1. You can go there for breakfast, lunch, or dinner.
2. Many people order hamburgers there.
3. People go there when they're in a hurry.

FAST-FOOD RESTAURANT

Name That Place!

1. People sit there.
2. People sometimes laugh or cry there.
3. People watch movies there.

MOVIE THEATER

Name That Place!

1. This place is for women.
2. Women buy special clothes there.
3. Women go there when they're going to have a baby.

MATERNITY SHOP

Name That Place!

1. You go there with your car.
2. Someone can fix your car there.
3. You go there to get gas.

GAS STATION/SERVICE STATION

Name That Place!

1. You often have to wait in line there.
2. You go there to send things.
3. You go there to buy stamps.

POST OFFICE

Name That Place!

1. People often go there with children.
2. You can buy games there.
3. You buy toys there.

TOY STORE

Name That Place!

1. You buy magazines there.
2. You buy newspapers there.
3. It's on the street.

NEWSSTAND

Name That Place!

1. You can sit and relax there.
2. People drink things there.
3. You can buy different kinds of coffee there.

COFFEE SHOP

Name That Place!

1. There are machines there.
2. People go there to lose weight.
3. People go there to exercise.

HEALTH CLUB

Places Around Town Board Game

- Put your markers on *Start.*
- Take turns tossing the Game Cube (or flipping a coin) to move your marker around the board.
- Follow the instructions in each space.

START

What are **2** places where you can buy food?

What are **2** places where you can buy clothing?

Pick a Guess-the-Place card! **Draw the item on the card.** Everyone has to guess the place associated with that item.

What are **2** places where you go when you're sick?

What are **3** places you can park your car?

Tell **3** places in your neighborhood. What are their names?

What are **2** places where you can get your hair cut?

Pick a Guess-the-Place card! **Draw the item on the card.** Everyone has to guess the place associated with that item.

You're going to **3** places: First, you're going to buy something. Then you're going to eat something. And then you're going to do something important. Where are you going? And what are you going to do there?

What's another word for child-care center? cleaner's? delicatessen? drug store? flower shop? eye-care center?

FINISH

You went to **3** places yesterday. Where did you go and what did you do there? Sing a song about it!

What's another word for . . . gas station? mall? pet shop? taxi? taxi driver? traffic light?

Draw a bill and coin. [bank]	Draw a book. [book store]	Draw a bus. [bus station]
Draw a car. [car dealership]	Draw a baby. [child-care center]	Draw a tie and jacket. [clothing store]
Draw a computer. [computer store]	Draw a donut. [donut shop]	Draw some flowers. [florist/flower shop]
Draw a chair and lamp. [furniture store]	Draw a woman's hairdo. [hair salon]	Draw a hammer. [hardware store]
Draw an ice cream cone. [ice cream shop]	Draw a musical note. [music store]	Draw a hand and fingernail. [nail salon]
Draw a letter with a stamp. [post office]	Draw a place setting. [restaurant]	Draw a pair of shoes. [shoe store]

- Spend 3 minutes looking very carefully at the people in each of the photographs.
- Put this Activity Master aside and complete Activity Master 51 to see how many of these differences you can remember.

Markov Family Photo

Pavlov Family Photo

- Answer the questions below based on the photographs on Activity Master 50.
- Look at Activity Master 50 again to check your answers. How well did you remember the differences?

1. Mrs. Markov is (tall   short), and Mrs. Pavlov is (tall   short).

2. Mr. Markov has a (beard   mustache), and Mr. Pavlov has a (beard   mustache).

3. The Markovs' older son is (thin   heavy), and the Pavlovs' older son is (thin   heavy).

4. The Markovs' younger son has (black   blond) hair, and the Pavlovs' younger son has (black   blond) hair.

5. The Markovs' older daughter has (straight   curly) hair, and the Pavlovs' older daughter has (straight   curly) hair.

6. The Markovs' younger daughter has (long   shoulder-length) hair, and the Pavlovs' younger daughter has (long   shoulder-length) hair.

7. Grandfather Markov is (average weight   heavy), and Grandfather Pavlov is (average weight   heavy).

8. Grandmother Markov is wearing (fancy   plain) clothes, and Grandmother Pavlov is wearing (fancy   plain) clothes.

9. The Markovs' dog is (large   small), and the Pavlovs' dog is (large   small).

- Put your markers on *Start.*
- Take turns tossing the Game Cube (or flipping a coin) to move your marker around the board.
- Follow the instructions in each space.

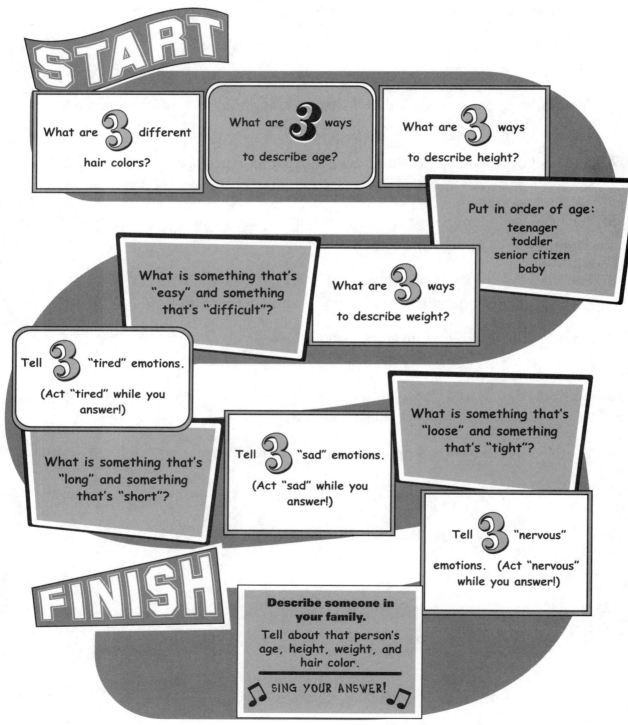

START

What are **3** different hair colors?

What are **3** ways to describe age?

What are **3** ways to describe height?

Put in order of age:
teenager
toddler
senior citizen
baby

What is something that's "easy" and something that's "difficult"?

What are **3** ways to describe weight?

Tell **3** "tired" emotions. (Act "tired" while you answer!)

What is something that's "loose" and something that's "tight"?

What is something that's "long" and something that's "short"?

Tell **3** "sad" emotions. (Act "sad" while you answer!)

Tell **3** "nervous" emotions. (Act "nervous" while you answer!)

FINISH

Describe someone in your family.
Tell about that person's age, height, weight, and hair color.
♪ SING YOUR ANSWER! ♪

Opposite Adjective Cards

OPPOSITES

The opposite of *big* is _____.

OPPOSITES

The opposite of *fast* is _____.

OPPOSITES

The opposite of *heavy* is _____.

OPPOSITES

The opposite of *dark* is _____.

OPPOSITES

The opposite of *high* is _____.

OPPOSITES

The opposite of *good* is _____.

OPPOSITES

The opposite of *loose* is _____.

OPPOSITES

The opposite of *smooth* is _____.

OPPOSITES

The opposite of *rich* is _____.

OPPOSITES

The opposite of *handsome* is _____.

OPPOSITES

The opposite of *wet* is _____.

OPPOSITES

The opposite of *shiny* is _____.

OPPOSITES

The opposite of *sharp* is _____.

OPPOSITES

The opposite of *honest* is _____.

OPPOSITES

The opposite of *comfortable* is _____.

OPPOSITES

The opposite of *curly* is _____.

OPPOSITES

The opposite of *straight* is _____.

OPPOSITES

The opposite of *easy* is _____.

PANTOMIME	PANTOMIME
"tired"	"sick"
PANTOMIME	PANTOMIME
"hot"	"cold"
PANTOMIME	PANTOMIME
"hungry"	"full"
PANTOMIME	PANTOMIME
"happy"	"sad"
PANTOMIME	PANTOMIME
"excited"	"disappointed"
PANTOMIME	PANTOMIME
"angry"	"surprised"
PANTOMIME	PANTOMIME
"nervous"	"scared"
PANTOMIME	PANTOMIME
"embarrassed"	"confused"
PANTOMIME	PANTOMIME
"bored"	"shocked"

DRAW	DRAW
tall & short	**young & old**
DRAW	DRAW
heavy & thin	**long & short**
DRAW	DRAW
full & empty	**large & small**
DRAW	DRAW
straight & crooked	**straight & curly**
DRAW	DRAW
wide & narrow	**thick & thin**
DRAW	DRAW
dark & light	**neat & messy**
DRAW	DRAW
married & single	**rich & poor**
DRAW	DRAW
pretty & ugly	**open & closed**
DRAW	DRAW
expensive & cheap	**fancy & plain**

- Work with a partner. (Don't look at your partner's paper.)
- Ask your partner questions to find out the prices of foods that are on sale at Mendoza's Market.
- Write the price next to each item.
- Compare your list with your partner's.

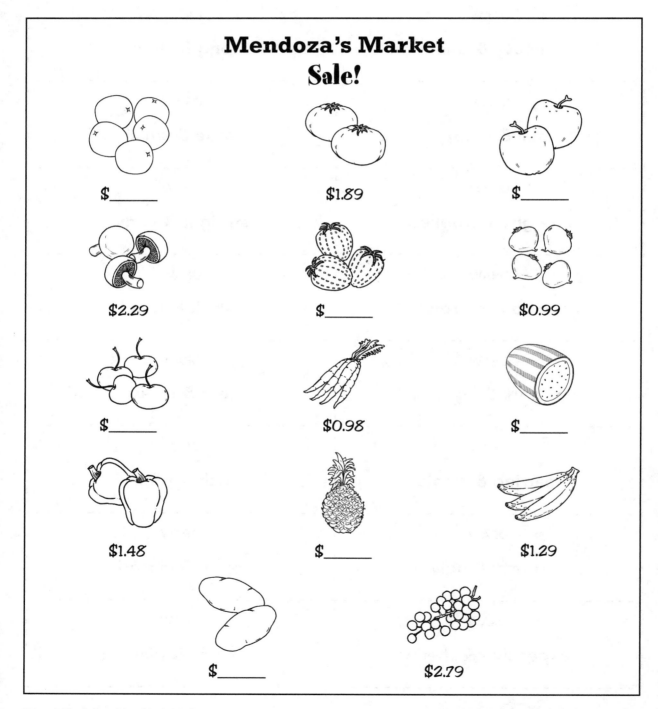

Mendoza's Market
Sale!

$_____ $1.89 $_____

$2.29 $_____ $0.99

$_____ $0.98 $_____

$1.48 $_____ $1.29

$_____ $2.79

- Work with a partner. (Don't look at your partner's paper.)
- Ask your partner questions to find out the prices of foods that are on sale at Mendoza's Market.
- Write the price next to each item.
- Compare your list with your partner's.

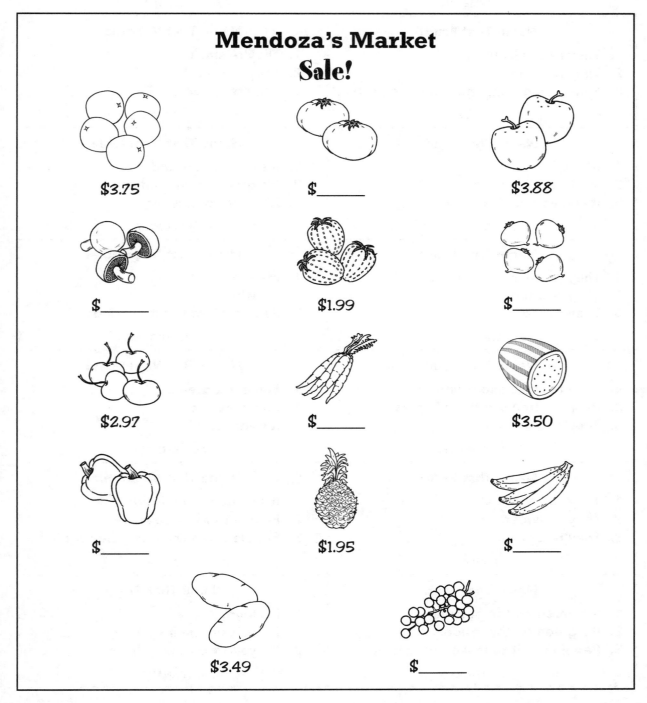

Mendoza's Market
Sale!

$3.75

$_____

$3.88

$_____

$1.99

$_____

$2.97

$_____

$3.50

$_____

$1.95

$_____

$3.49

$_____

Name That Fruit!

1. It's long.
2. It's green on the outside.
3. It's red on the inside.

WATERMELON

Name That Vegetable!

1. It's round.
2. It's green.
3. People use it in a salad.

LETTUCE

Name That Fruit!

1. They're small and round.
2. They're sweet.
3. Some are green, and some are purple.

GRAPES

Name That Vegetable!

1. They're small.
2. They're round.
3. They're green.

PEAS

Name That Fruit!

1. It's yellow.
2. It's sweet.
3. It comes from Hawaii.

PINEAPPLE

Name That Vegetable!

1. It's long and round.
2. It's green on the outside.
3. It's white on the inside.

CUCUMBER

Name That Fruit!

1. They're small and round.
2. They're sweet.
3. They're red.

CHERRIES

Name That Vegetable!

1. It's soft.
2. It's white.
3. People often put it in salads.

MUSHROOM

Name That Fruit!

1. They're small and round.
2. People often use them in pies.
3. They're blue.

BLUEBERRIES

Name That Vegetable!

1. Some are green.
2. Some are red.
3. It's very spicy.

JALAPEÑO PEPPER

Name That Fruit!

1. They're very small.
2. They're sweet.
3. They're brown.

RAISINS

Name That Vegetable!

1. It's white on the inside.
2. People put it in salads.
3. People often cry when they cut it.

ONION

Name That Fruit!

1. It's green on the outside.
2. It's green on the inside.
3. People use it to make guacamole.

AVOCADO

Name That Fruit!

1. It's long.
2. It's soft on the inside.
3. It's yellow on the outside.

BANANA

- Work with a partner. Look at what these people bought at the supermarket.
- There are eight differences between what Shirley and Charlie bought.
- Talk with your partner about the differences and write them in the chart below.

Shirley bought . . .	Charlie bought . . .
1. a pound of chicken	**1.** a pound of ground beef
2.	**2.**
3.	**3.**
4.	**4.**
5.	**5.**
6.	**6.**
7.	**7.**
8.	**8.**

- Work with a partner. Look at what these people bought at the supermarket.
- There are eight differences between what Shirley and Charlie bought.
- Talk with your partner about the differences and write them in the chart below.

Shirley bought . . .	Charlie bought . . .
1. a pound of chicken	**1.** a pound of ground beef
2.	**2.**
3.	**3.**
4.	**4.**
5.	**5.**
6.	**6.**
7.	**7.**
8.	**8.**

Draw an apple. Can your team guess what fruit this is?	Draw a watermelon. Can your team guess what fruit this is?	Draw a banana. Can your team guess what fruit this is?	Draw a mushroom. Can your team guess what vegetable this is?
Draw some lettuce. Can your team guess what vegetable this is?	Draw a piece of corn. Can your team guess what vegetable this is?	What are two fruits or vegetables that begin with the letter "a"?	What are three vegetables that being with the letter "c"?
What is a fruit that's green, a vegetable that's red, and a fruit that's purple?	What are two kinds of berries?	You're making a vegetable salad. What are five vegetables you put in your salad?	What are three kinds of juice?
What are two kinds of cheese you buy at the deli counter?	What are two snack foods?	What are two canned goods?	What are two kinds of baked goods?
Name two paper products.	Name two people who work in the supermarket.	What are two things you can buy in a bag?	What are two things you can buy in a box?
What are two things you can buy in a can?	What are two things you can buy in a container?	What are two things you can buy in a bottle?	What are two things you can buy in a gallon?

Draw a pineapple. Can your team guess what fruit this is?	Draw some grapes. Can your team guess what fruit this is?	Draw some strawberries. Can your team guess what fruit this is?	Draw a carrot. Can your team guess what vegetable this is?
Draw an onion. Can your team guess what vegetable this is?	Tell three fruits that are red.	What are three fruits that begin with the letter "p"?	What is a fruit that's yellow, a vegetable that's orange, and a fruit that's red?
What are five vegetables that are green?	You're making a fruit salad. What are five fruits you put in your salad?	What are three dairy products?	What are two kinds of deli meat?
Name two frozen foods.	Name two packaged goods.	Name three condiments.	What is a common baking product?
Name two baby products.	Name a machine you find in a supermarket.	What are two things you can buy in a bottle?	What are two things you can buy in a bunch?
What are two things you can buy in a carton?	What are two things you can buy in a head?	What are two things you can buy in a pint?	What are two things you can buy in a pound?

Add _____.

Bake _____.

Barbecue _____.

Boil _____.

Broil _____.

Chop _____.

Cut _____.

Fry _____.

Grate _____.

Peel _____.

Pour _____.

Slice _____.

Steam _____.

Stir _____.

Stir-fry _____.

DRAW bowl	DRAW colander	DRAW double boiler
DRAW egg beater	DRAW frying pan	DRAW ice cream scoop
DRAW knife	DRAW ladle	DRAW measuring cup
DRAW pot	DRAW rolling pin	DRAW spatula
DRAW strainer	DRAW whisk	DRAW wok

How many teaspoons are in a tablespoon?

How many tablespoons are in one fluid ounce?

How many ounces are in a cup?

How many ounces are in a pint?

How many ounces are in a quart?

How many ounces are in a gallon?

How many ounces are in a quarter of a pound?

How many ounces are in half a pound?

How many ounces are in three-quarters of a pound?

How many ounces are in a pound?

How many pints are in a quart?

Put in order:
quart
pint
gallon
cup

Give a recipe for fruit punch with three ingredients and the amounts.

- Put your markers on *Start.*
- Take turns tossing the Game Cube (or flipping a coin) to move your marker around the board.
- Follow the instructions in each space.

START

What are **2** things you can order in a fast-food restaurant?

What are **2** kinds of sandwiches you can order in a sandwich shop?

What are **2** appetizers on a restaurant menu?

What are **2** things you can order for breakfast in a coffee shop?

What are **2** desserts on a restaurant menu?

What's your favorite dessert in a fast-food restaurant?

SING A SONG ABOUT IT!

What are **2** condiments you can find in a fast-food restaurant?

What are **2** entrees on a restaurant menu?

True or False? The knife goes to the left of the dinner plate.

What are **2** kinds of bread you can use to make a sandwich?

What are **2** side dishes on a restaurant menu?

What are **2** kinds of salads on a restaurant menu?

True or False? The napkin goes under the fork.

FINISH

You work in a restaurant. Tell something you do at work. Your classmates have to guess your job.

What are **2** kinds of plates in a place setting?

7.7   *Restaurant Board Game*
BOARD GAME
Word by Word Communication Games & Activity Masters, Page 37

- Ask other students what items of clothing they have.
- When you find someone who has the item on your grid, have that person write his or her name in that square.
- The first student with the most signatures with the game.

A Black Shirt? Name _____	Jeans? Name _____	A Gold Necklace? Name _____
A Blue Jacket? Name _____	An Umbrella? Name _____	Green Mittens? Name _____
Sunglasses? Name _____	White Slippers? Name _____	Boxer Shorts? Name _____
Black Leather Boots? Name _____	Flip-Flops? Name _____	Work Boots? Name _____
A Brown Wallet? Name _____	Pantyhose? Name _____	A Silver Bracelet? Name _____

- Work with a partner. (Don't look at your partner's paper.)
- Ask your partner questions to find out the prices of items that are on sale at Kovak's Department Store.
- Write the price next to each item.
- Compare your list with your partner's.

Kovak's Department Store
Sale!

$_____

$27.50

$_____

$11.00

$_____

$7.99

$_____

$26.00

$_____

$44.50

$_____

$19.99

$_____

$15.50

- Work with a partner. (Don't look at your partner's paper.)
- Ask your partner questions to find out the prices of items that are on sale at Kovak's Department Store.
- Write the price next to each item.
- Compare your list with your partner's.

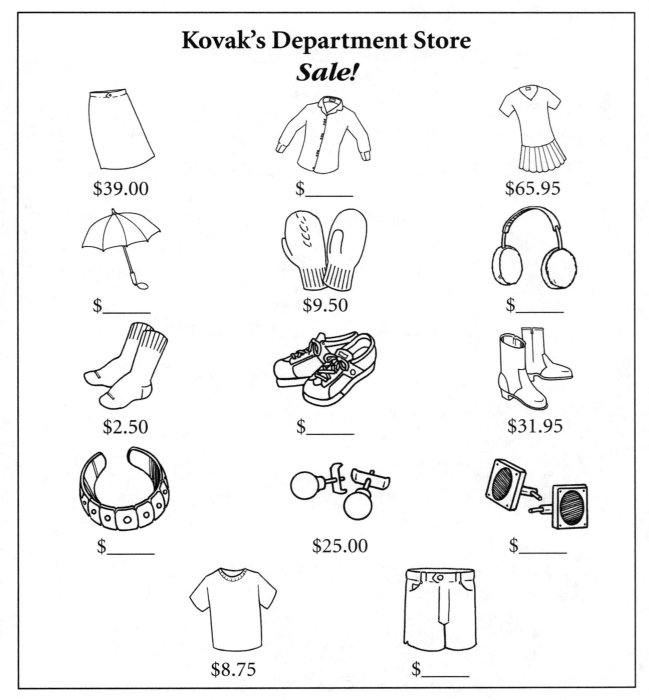

Kovak's Department Store
Sale!

$39.00 $_____ $65.95

$_____ $9.50 $_____

$2.50 $_____ $31.95

$_____ $25.00 $_____

$8.75 $_____

- Put your markers on *Start.*
- Take turns tossing the Game Cube (or flipping a coin) to move your marker around the board.
- Follow the instructions in each space.

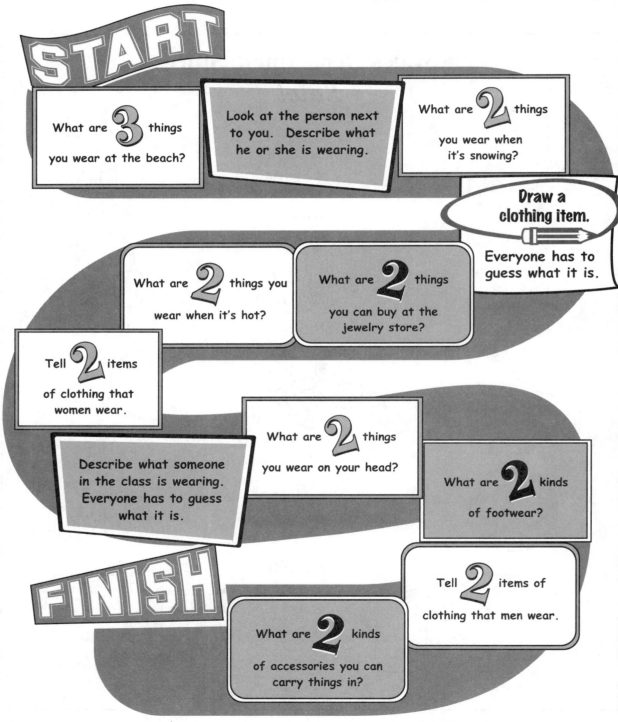

START

What are **3** things you wear at the beach?

Look at the person next to you. Describe what he or she is wearing.

What are **2** things you wear when it's snowing?

Draw a clothing item.
Everyone has to guess what it is.

What are **2** things you wear when it's hot?

What are **2** things you can buy at the jewelry store?

Tell **2** items of clothing that women wear.

Describe what someone in the class is wearing. Everyone has to guess what it is.

What are **2** things you wear on your head?

What are **2** kinds of footwear?

Tell **2** items of clothing that men wear.

FINISH

What are **2** kinds of accessories you can carry things in?

8.4 *Clothing Board Game I*
BOARD GAME
Word by Word Communication Games & Activity Masters, Page 41

Clothing Word Clue Cards

Name That Clothing Item!

1. Men wear it.
2. They wear it for very special occasions.
3. Many men wear it when they get married.

TUXEDO

Name That Clothing Item!

1. It can be long or short.
2. Women usually wear it.
3. They often wear it with a blouse or sweater.

SKIRT

Name That Accessory!

1. Men and women wear it.
2. It's long.
3. It goes around the waist.

BELT

Name That Outerwear Item!

1. It opens up.
2. It's round.
3. You use it when it's raining.

UMBRELLA

Name That Clothing Item!

1. Everybody wears them.
2. They're a type of pants.
3. They're usually blue.

JEANS

Name That Sleepwear Item!

1. They have a top and a bottom.
2. Men and women wear them.
3. You wear them when you go to bed.

PAJAMAS

Name That Outerwear Item!

1. You wear them when it's cold.
2. They keep you warm.
3. You wear them on your hands.

MITTENS

Name That Accessory!

1. Men and women carry it.
2. It can lock.
3. You carry important papers in it.

BRIEFCASE

Name That Clothing Item!

1. Only women wear it.
2. They wear it for a few months.
3. They wear it when they're going to have a baby.

MATERNITY DRESS

Name That Jewelry Item!

1. Men buy them.
2. Women wear them.
3. When a man gives it to a woman, he sometimes gets down on one knee.

ENGAGEMENT RING

Name That Accessory!

1. It holds a lot of things.
2. Students often use them.
3. You carry it on your back.

BACKPACK

Name That Clothing Item!

1. Men wear them.
2. They often wear them for special occasions.
3. They have three pieces.

THREE-PIECE SUIT

Name That Sleepwear Item!

1. You wear it in the morning and evening.
2. Men and women wear it.
3. You wear it over your pajamas.

BATHROBE

Name That Outerwear Item!

1. You wear it on your head.
2. It keeps your head dry.
3. You wear it when it's raining.

RAIN HAT

- Work with a partner. Look at each other's photos.
- There are eight differences between The Brady Family Photo A and the Brady Family Photo B. How are the following different—Ben Brady's shirt, Grandpa's tie, Grandma's sweater, Sally's T-shirt, Mary's pants, Bobby's shirt, Mrs. Brady's blouse, and Mr. Brady's jacket?
- Talk with your partner about the differences and write them in the chart below.

In the Brady Family Photo A	In the Brady Family Photo B
1. Ben is wearing a short-sleeved shirt.	**1.** Ben is wearing a long-sleeved shirt.
2.	**2.**
3.	**3.**
4.	**4.**
5.	**5.**
6.	**6.**
7.	**7.**
8.	**8.**

- Work with a partner. Look at each other's photos.
- There are eight differences between The Brady Family Photo A and the Brady Family Photo B. How are the following different—Ben Brady's shirt, Grandpa's tie, Grandma's sweater, Sally's T-shirt, Mary's pants, Bobby's shirt, Mrs. Brady's blouse, and Mr. Brady's jacket?
- Talk with your partner about the differences and write them in the chart below.

In the Brady Family Photo A	In the Brady Family Photo B
1. Ben is wearing a short-sleeved shirt.	**1.** Ben is wearing a long-sleeved shirt.
2.	**2.**
3.	**3.**
4.	**4.**
5.	**5.**
6.	**6.**
7.	**7.**
8.	**8.**

- Put your markers on *Start.*
- Take turns tossing the Game Cube (or flipping a coin) to move your marker around the board.
- Follow the instructions in each space.

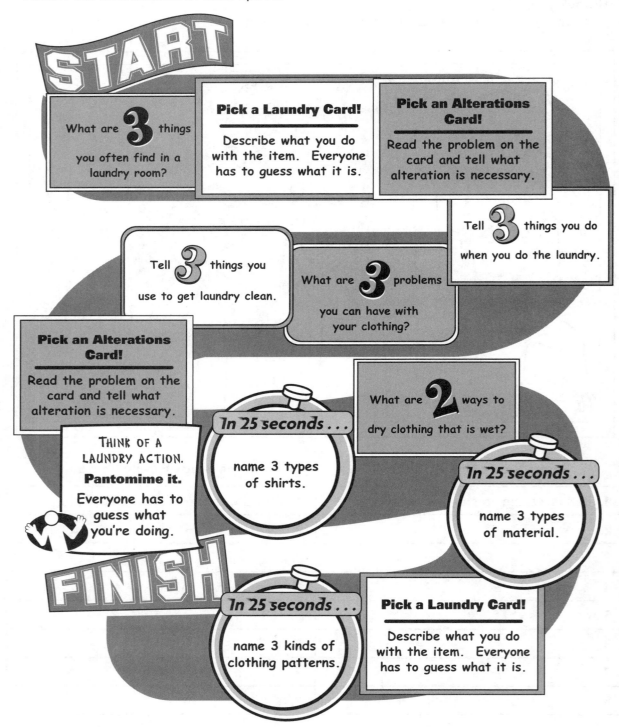

START

What are **3** things you often find in a laundry room?

Pick a Laundry Card!
Describe what you do with the item. Everyone has to guess what it is.

Pick an Alterations Card!
Read the problem on the card and tell what alteration is necessary.

Tell **3** things you do when you do the laundry.

Tell **3** things you use to get laundry clean.

What are **3** problems you can have with your clothing?

Pick an Alterations Card!
Read the problem on the card and tell what alteration is necessary.

What are **2** ways to dry clothing that is wet?

THINK OF A LAUNDRY ACTION. **Pantomime it.** Everyone has to guess what you're doing.

In 25 seconds . . . name 3 types of shirts.

In 25 seconds . . . name 3 types of material.

FINISH

In 25 seconds . . . name 3 kinds of clothing patterns.

Pick a Laundry Card!
Describe what you do with the item. Everyone has to guess what it is.

LAUNDRY CARD

What do you do with it?

washing machine

LAUNDRY CARD

What do you do with it?

dryer

LAUNDRY CARD

What do you do with it?

detergent

LAUNDRY CARD

What do you do with it?

bleach

LAUNDRY CARD

What do you do with it?

fabric softener

LAUNDRY CARD

What do you do with it?

clothespin

LAUNDRY CARD

What do you do with it?

laundry basket

ALTERATIONS CARD

Barbara's skirt is too long.
What should she do?

ALTERATIONS CARD

Emily grew three inches last summer.
Some of her skirts are too short.
What should she do?

ALTERATIONS CARD

The buttonholes on my collar are too
loose. What should I do?

ALTERATIONS CARD

Susan lost a lot of weight and now
her clothes are too big.
What should she do?

ALTERATIONS CARD

Peter gained a lot of weight and now
his clothes are too tight.
What should he do?

- Work with a partner. (Don't look at your partner's paper.)
- Ask your partner questions to find out the birthdays of members of the Kim family and what presents they would like.
- Write the birthday and the gift item next to the person's name.
- Compare answers with your partner.

Birthday	Name	Present
	Amy Kim	
February 23rd	Mrs. Kim	a digital camera
	Grandmother Kim	
May 31st	Aunt Elizabeth	a personal CD player
	Allison Kim	
September 22nd	David Kim	a skateboard
	Mr. Kim	
November 25th	Uncle William	a fax machine
	Grandfather Kim	

- Work with a partner. (Don't look at your partner's paper.)
- Ask your partner questions to find out the birthdays of members of the Kim family and what presents they would like.
- Write the birthday and the gift item next to the person's name.
- Compare answers with your partner.

Birthday	Name	Present
January 18th	Amy Kim	a DVD player
	Mrs. Kim	
April 12th	Grandmother Kim	a portable TV
	Aunt Elizabeth	
August 3rd	Allison Kim	a doll house
	David Kim	
October 21st	Mr. Kim	a camcorder
	Uncle William	
December 16th	Grandfather Kim	a cell phone

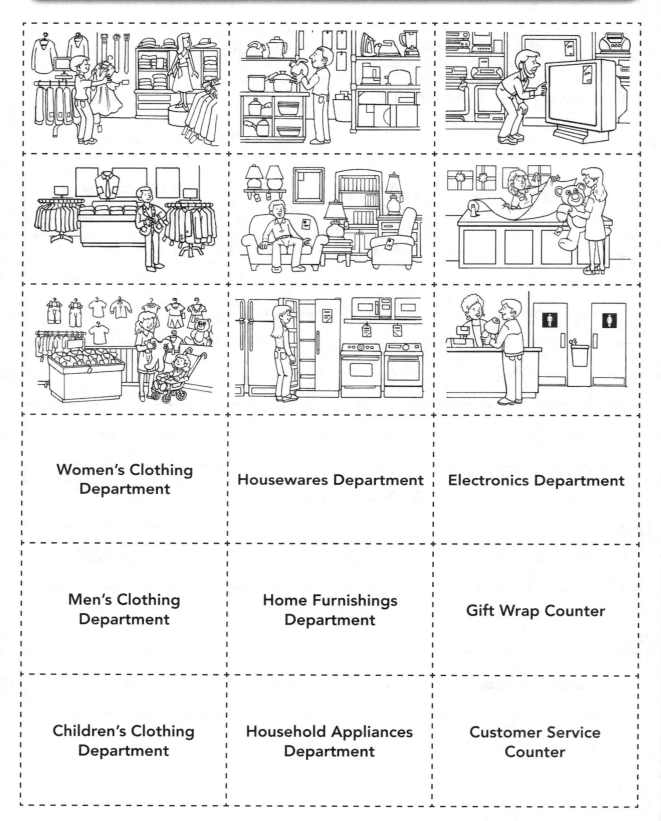

Women's Clothing Department	**Housewares Department**	**Electronics Department**
Men's Clothing Department	**Home Furnishings Department**	**Gift Wrap Counter**
Children's Clothing Department	**Household Appliances Department**	**Customer Service Counter**

9.2   *Department Store Concentration Game*
CONCENTRATION GAME
Word by Word Communication Games & Activity Masters, Page 46

What's in Your Home?

- Ask other students what things they have in their home.
- When you find someone who has the item on your grid, have that person write his or her name in that square.
- The first student with the most signatures with the game.

A Plasma TV? Name _____	**A Video Camera?** Name _____	**A CD Player?** Name _____
A Stereo System? Name _____	**A Cordless Phone?** Name _____	**A Digital Camera?** Name _____
An Answering Machine? Name _____	**A Desktop Computer?** Name _____	**A Computer Game?** Name _____
A Printer? Name _____	**A Board Game?** Name _____	**Crayons?** Name _____
A Doll House? Name _____	**A Skateboard?** Name _____	**A Hula Hoop?** Name _____

Birthday Match Cards

82

My name is Jessie.
My birthday is April 2nd.
I want a CD player.
I also want a bicycle.

My name is Jessie.
My birthday is April 2nd.
I want a CD player.
I also want a radio.

My name is Tracy.
My birthday is September 23rd.
I want a desktop computer.
I also want a digital camera.

My name is Tracy.
My birthday is September 23rd.
I want a desktop computer.
I also want a zoom lens.

My name is Alex.
My birthday is October 11th.
I want a cordless phone.
I also want a board game.

My name is Alex.
My birthday is October 11th.
I want a cordless phone.
I also want a video game.

My name is Pat.
My birthday is January 5th.
I want a rubber ball.
I also want a train set.

My name is Pat.
My birthday is January 5th.
I want a rubber ball.
I also want a racing car set.

My name is Chris.
My birthday is May 1st.
I want an LCD screen.
I also want a surge protector.

My name is Chris.
My birthday is May 1st.
I want an LCD screen.
I also want a printer.

My name is Lee.
My birthday is November 22nd.
I want a computer game.
I also want a CD player.

My name is Lee.
My birthday is November 22nd.
I want a computer game.
I also want a DVD player.

My name is Kim.
My birthday is December 6th.
I want a turntable.
I also want a camcorder.

My name is Kim.
My birthday is December 6th.
I want a turntable.
I also want a cell phone.

9.4 *Birthday Match Game*
MATCHING GAME
Word by Word Communication Games & Activity Masters, Page 48

© 2010 Pearson Education
Duplication for classroom use is permitted.© 2010 Pearson Education
Duplication for classroom use is permitted.

- Put your markers on *Start.*
- Take turns tossing the Game Cube (or flipping a coin) to move your marker around the board.
- Follow the instructions in each space.

START

What are **2** different types of TVs?

Tell **3** things on a sales receipt.

Name **3** items in the video department.

Pick a Shopping Game Mime Card!
Pantomime how to use the item. Everyone has to guess what it is.

Name **3** parts of a stereo system.

Name **3** things in a toy store that begin with the letter "c."

Name **3** items in the camera department.

Pick a Shopping Game Mime Card!
Pantomime how to use the item. Everyone has to guess what it is.

Name **3** items in the audio department.

Name **3** things in a toy store.

Name **3** things in a toy store that you can ride.

FINISH

What are **3** items in a desktop computer system?

Pick a Shopping Game Mime Card!
Pantomime how to use the item. Everyone has to guess what it is.

bicycle	bubble soap	calculator
camera	CD player	cell phone
coloring book and crayons	fax machine	hand-held video system
headphones	hula hoop	jump rope
keyboard	microphone	mouse
puzzle	rubber ball	train set

Would YOU rather buy . . . ?	Would your partner rather buy . . . ?
☐ a plasma TV?	☐ a plasma TV?
☐ an LCD TV?	☐ an LCD TV?
☐ a VCR?	☐ a VCR?
☐ a DVD?	☐ a DVD?
☐ a cordless phone?	☐ a cordless phone?
☐ a cell phone?	☐ a cell phone?
☐ a clock radio?	☐ a clock radio?
☐ a shortwave radio?	☐ a shortwave radio?
☐ a board game?	☐ a board game?
☐ a jigsaw puzzle?	☐ a jigsaw puzzle?
☐ a turntable?	☐ a turntable?
☐ a CD player?	☐ a CD player?
☐ a fax machine?	☐ a fax machine?
☐ a scanner?	☐ a scanner?
☐ a 35 millimeter camera?	☐ a 35 millimeter camera?
☐ a digital camera?	☐ a digital camera?
☐ a desktop computer?	☐ a desktop computer?
☐ a notebook computer?	☐ a notebook computer?
☐ a mouse?	☐ a mouse?
☐ a trackball?	☐ a trackball?
☐ crayons?	☐ crayons?
☐ magic markers?	☐ magic markers?
☐ a computer game?	☐ a computer game?
☐ an educational software program?	☐ an educational software program?

- Work in groups of three.
- Student A picks one of the following cards and reads the situation.
- Student B gives advice, then Student C reacts to the advice.
- The group should then discuss each situation and decide on the best advice.
- For the next problem, Student B picks the card. Student C gives advice, and Student A reacts. Continue switching roles until all the problem situations have been discussed.
- Report the group's conclusions to the class.

Melanie found a dress she loves, and it's on sale for 75% off the regular price. However, last week she said to her roommate, "I promise I won't buy any new clothes for six months!" What should Melanie do?

Amy Anderson is going to college in September. Her parents offered to buy her a desktop computer, but Amy wants a laptop. Unfortunately, the laptop is more expensive than the desktop. What should Amy do?

Mr. Carter loves to watch sports on TV. However, his wife hates sports and thinks TV is a waste of time. There's a 50-inch plasma TV on sale at Ace Electronics. Mr. Carter really wants to buy it. What should he do?

Rosa Gomez is 10 years old. She wants a cell phone. Mrs. Gomez thinks it's a good idea to buy Rosa a cell phone. However, Mr. Gomez thinks it's a bad idea. What should Mr. and Mrs. Gomez do?

John Harris is 16 years old. He lost his cell phone for the third time this year. He thinks his parents should buy him another phone. His parents say that this time John should pay for the cell phone himself. John is upset. What should the Harris family do?

Mrs. Lewis took her five-year-old daughter, Cindy, to the toy store to buy her a new doll. Mrs. Lewis had no idea that while they were at the toy store, Cindy put a stuffed animal in her coat pocket and brought it home. What should Mrs. Lewis do?

Amanda Lee is in college. She gets good grades, but she doesn't have much money for clothes or to do things with her friends. She has the chance to take a full-time job in the Women's Clothing Department at a local department store. If she takes the job, she'll have to take fewer classes and she'll graduate from college a year late. What should she do?

Roger Peterson bought a 35 millimeter camera, a zoom lens, a tripod, and a camera case at Waldo's Camera Shop. Two months later, the camera stopped working. Roger was extremely upset. He went back to Waldo's Camera Shop, but the salesperson said to him, "Sorry, Mr. Peterson, but there's nothing we can do to help you." What should Roger do?

- Ask other students what they did at the bank last month.
- When you find someone who did the activity on your grid, have that person write his or her name in that square.
- The first student with the most signatures with the game.

Make a Deposit? Name _____	**Make a Withdrawal?** Name _____	**Fill Out a Deposit Slip?** Name _____
Use an ATM? Name _____	**Talk with a Bank Teller?** Name _____	**Write a Check?** Name _____
Balance Your Checkbook? Name _____	**Open a Bank Account?** Name _____	**Pay a Credit Card Bill?** Name _____
Make a Car Payment? Name _____	**Make a Rent Payment?** Name _____	**Pay a Cable TV Bill?** Name _____

Banking & Finance Board Game

89

- Put your markers on *Start.*
- Take turns tossing the Game Cube (or flipping a coin) to move your marker around the board.
- Follow the instructions in each space.

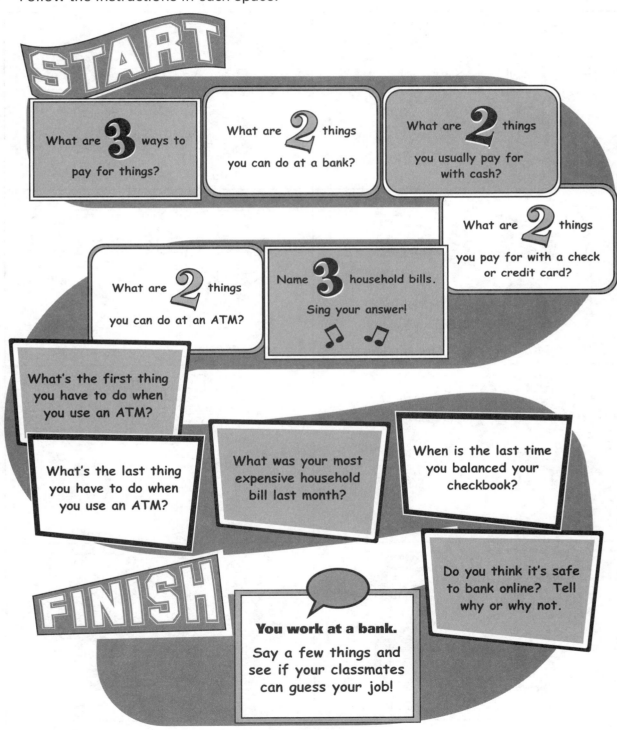

START

What are **3** ways to pay for things?

What are **2** things you can do at a bank?

What are **2** things you usually pay for with cash?

What are **2** things you pay for with a check or credit card?

What are **2** things you can do at an ATM?

Name **3** household bills. Sing your answer! ♫ ♫

What's the first thing you have to do when you use an ATM?

What's the last thing you have to do when you use an ATM?

What was your most expensive household bill last month?

When is the last time you balanced your checkbook?

FINISH

You work at a bank. Say a few things and see if your classmates can guess your job!

Do you think it's safe to bank online? Tell why or why not.

10.3 *Banking & Finance Board Game*
BOARD GAME
Word by Word Communication Games & Activity Masters, Page 54

© 2010 Pearson Education
Duplication for classroom use is permitted.

They Did Different Things

90

- Spend 3 minutes looking very carefully at each of the following pairs of pictures.
- Put this Activity Master away and complete Activity Master 91 to see how many of these differences you can remember.

Omar   Owen   Rita   Brigitta

Mrs. Lee   Mrs. McGee   Randy   Andy

Ricardo   Bernardo   Keiko   Reiko

Judy   Julie   Gino   Dino

10.4 *Post Office & Library Memory Challenge*
MEMORY GAME
Word by Word Communication Games & Activity Masters, Page 55

- Answer the questions below based on the illustrations on Activity Master 90.
- Look at Activity Master 90 again to check your answers. How well did you remember the differences?

1. Omar went to the post office and mailed (a letter   a package).

2. Owen also went to the post office. He mailed (a letter   a package).

3. Brigitta went to the post office at 8 o'clock this morning and bought a
   (sheet of stamps   roll of stamps).

4. Rita went to the post office and bought a (sheet of stamps   roll of stamps).

5. Mrs. Lee went to the post office today and sent a package to her sister
   (priority mail   express mail).

6. Mrs. McGee also went to the post office today. She mailed a package
   (priority mail   express mail).

7. Randy went to the library on Saturday afternoon and looked through the
   (online catalog   card catalog).

8. Andy also went to the library on Saturday afternoon. He looked through the
   (online catalog   card catalog).

9. Bernardo went to the library this morning. He looked for information in the
   (reference section   media section).

10. Ricardo also went to the library this morning. He looked for information in the
    (reference section   media section).

11. Keiko went to the library and looked at (CDs   books on tape).

12. Reiko also went to the library. She looked at (CDs   books on tape).

13. Judy went to the library and read some (newspapers   magazines).

14. Julie went to the library and read some (newspapers   magazines).

15. Gino went to the library today and looked up information in the
    (encyclopedia   dictionary).

16. Dino also went to the library today. He looked up information in the
    (encyclopedia   dictionary).

- Work with a partner.
- In the statements below, circle the information that is true about yourself.
- Then take turns reading your statements to your partner. If your answers are the same, you earn a point. If your answers are different, you don't earn any points.
- After you have completed all the statements, report to the class how many points you have. The winning pair should then share their matching statements with the class.

1. (I take   I don't take) my letters to the post office.

2. (I buy   I don't buy) stamps at the post office.

3. (I know   I don't know) the name of my mail carrier.

4. (I mailed   I didn't mail) an express mail envelope this month.

5. (I always   I never) write my return address on the letters I send.

6. (I filled out   I didn't fill out) a change-of-address form when I moved.

7. (I like to   I don't like to) collect stamps from different countries.

8. (I have   I don't have) a library card.

9. (I like to   I don't like to) read the newspaper in English.

10. (I like to   I don't like to) listen to books on tape.

11. (I know how to use   I don't know how to use) a microfilm reader.

12. (I like to   I don't like to) read magazines at the library.

13. (I went   I didn't go) to the library this week.

14. (I know   I don't know) the location of the library in my neighborhood.

15. (I often   I sometimes   I never) ask the reference librarian a question.

16. (I borrow   I don't borrow) DVDs from the library.

- Work with a partner.
- Ask your partner questions about what happened in Brookdale yesterday.
- Write the answers in the chart below.
- Compare events with your partner.

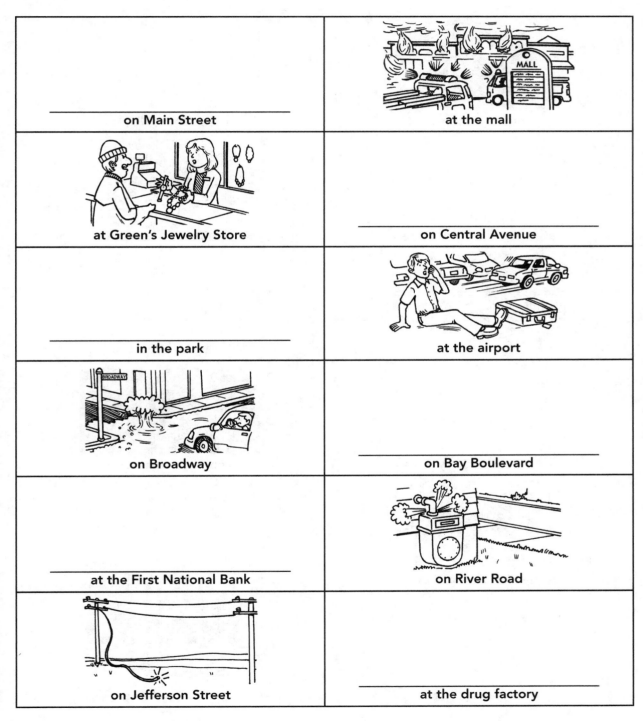

_____ on Main Street	at the mall
at Green's Jewelry Store	_____ on Central Avenue
_____ in the park	at the airport
on Broadway	_____ on Bay Boulevard
_____ at the First National Bank	on River Road
on Jefferson Street	_____ at the drug factory

- Work with a partner.
- Ask your partner questions about what happened in Brookdale yesterday.
- Write the answers in the chart below.
- Compare events with your partner.

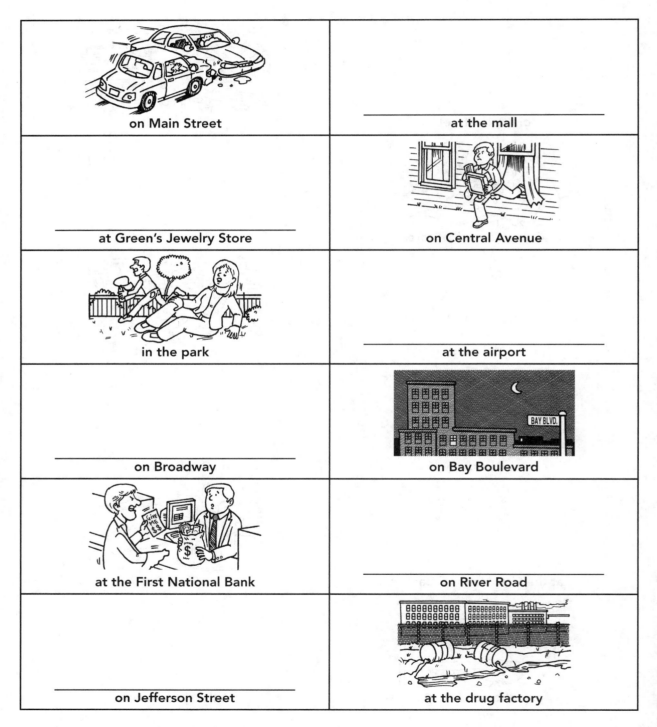

on Main Street	at the mall
at Green's Jewelry Store	on Central Avenue
in the park	at the airport
on Broadway	on Bay Boulevard
at the First National Bank	on River Road
on Jefferson Street	at the drug factory

BAY BLVD.

Community Life Board Game

- Put your markers on *Start.*
- Take turns tossing the Game Cube (or flipping a coin) to move your marker around the board.
- Follow the instructions in each space.

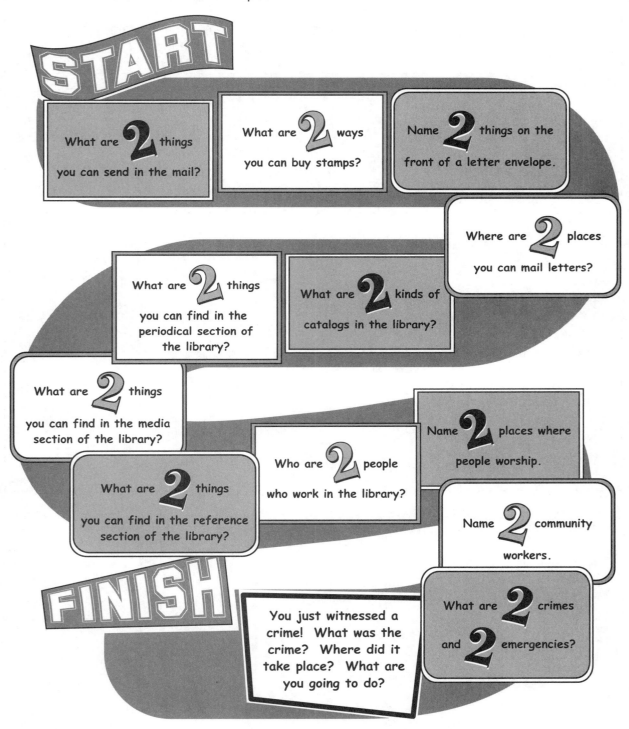

© 2010 Pearson Education
Duplication for classroom use is permitted.

2 eyes	**3** ears	**4** mouth
5 nose	**6** hair	**7** eyebrows
8 neck	**9** chest	**10** abdomen
11 arms	**12** legs	

- Put your markers on *Start.*
- Take turns tossing the Game Cube (or flipping a coin) to move your marker around the board.
- Follow the instructions in each space.

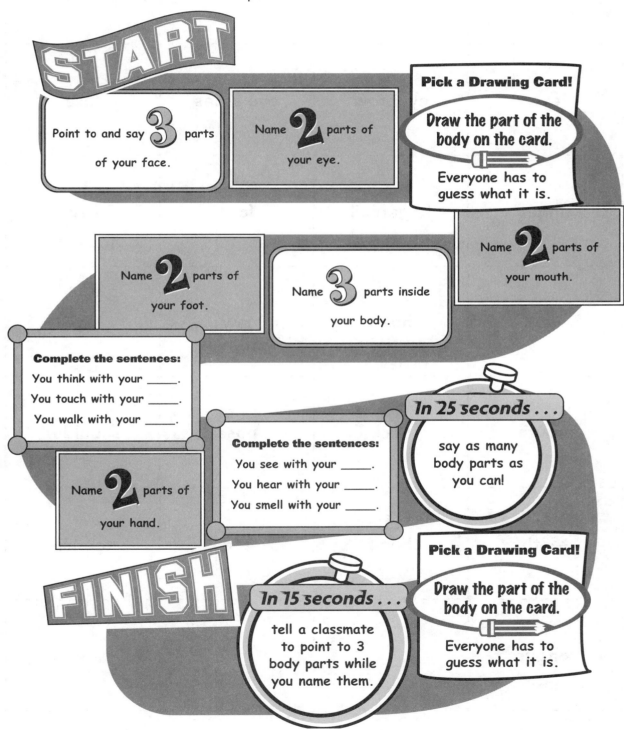

START

Point to and say **3** parts of your face.

Name **2** parts of your eye.

Pick a Drawing Card!
Draw the part of the body on the card.
Everyone has to guess what it is.

Name **2** parts of your mouth.

Name **2** parts of your foot.

Name **3** parts inside your body.

Complete the sentences:
You think with your _____.
You touch with your _____.
You walk with your _____.

In 25 seconds . . .
say as many body parts as you can!

Name **2** parts of your hand.

Complete the sentences:
You see with your _____.
You hear with your _____.
You smell with your _____.

FINISH

In 15 seconds . . .
tell a classmate to point to 3 body parts while you name them.

Pick a Drawing Card!
Draw the part of the body on the card.
Everyone has to guess what it is.

ankle	arm	ear	elbow
eye	eyebrow	eyelashes	face
finger	fingernail	foot	hair
hand	head	jaw	lip
mouth	neck	nose	shoulder
teeth	thumb	toe	toenail
tongue			

- Spend 3 minutes looking very carefully at each of the following pairs of pictures.
- Put this Activity Master aside and complete Activity Master 100 to see how many of these differences you can remember.

Ronaldo	Donaldo	Soo	Marylou
Eileen	Irene	Sasha	Natasha
Kim	Tim	Amanda	Miranda
Julie	Judy	Ahmed	Alfred
Len	Ken	Mrs. Sato	Mrs. Kato

11.3 *Ailment & Injury Memory Challenge*
MEMORY GAME
Word by Word Communication Games & Activity Masters, Page 61

- Answer the questions below based on the illustrations on Activity Master 99.
- Look at Activity Master 99 again to check your answers. How well did you remember the differences?

1. Ronaldo has a (cold   cough), and Donaldo has a (cold   cough).

2. Marylou has (an earache   a toothache), and her friend Soo has (an earache   a toothache).

3. Eileen is (itchy   swollen), and Irene is (itchy   swollen).

4. Sasha is (bloated   congested), and Natasha is (bloated   congested).

5. Tim has a broken (leg   arm), and Kim has a broken (leg   arm).

6. Amanda has a (stomachache   headache), and Miranda has a (stomachache   headache).

7. Judy has (measles   mumps), and Julie has (measles   mumps).

8. Alfred has (frostbite   heatstroke), and Ahmed has (frostbite   heatstroke).

9. Len has the (hiccups   chills), and Ken has the (hiccups   chills).

10. Mrs. Kato has a sprained (elbow   ankle), and Mrs. Sato has a sprained (elbow   ankle).

- Work with a partner. (Don't show this form to your partner.)
- Ask your partner questions about illnesses and emergencies in Max Miller's life:
  - A. What happened to Max when he was _____ years old?
  - B. He had/got _____.
- Write the illnesses and emergencies your partner tells you.
- Compare medical histories with your partner.

Max Miller's Medical History
age 5: mumps
age 6:
age 8: measles
age 10:
age 15: allergic reaction
age 30:
age 38: ear infection
age 45:
age 50: depression
age 65:

- Work with a partner. (Don't show this form to your partner.)
- Ask your partner questions about illnesses and emergencies in Max Miller's life:
    - A. What happened to Max when he was _____ years old?
    - B. He had/got _____.
- Write the illnesses and emergencies your partner tells you.
- Compare medical histories with your partner.

Max Miller's Medical History
age 5:
age 6: chicken pox
age 8:
age 10: strep throat
age 15:
age 30: diabetes
age 38:
age 45: heart disease
age 50:
age 65: heart attack

What Should They Do?

- Work in groups of three.
- Student A picks one of the following cards and reads the situation.
- Student B gives advice, then Student C reacts to the advice.
- The group should then discuss each situation and decide on the best advice.
- For the next problem, Student B picks the card. Student C gives advice, and Student A reacts. Continue switching roles until all the problem situations have been discussed.
- Report the group's conclusions to the class.

Mr. and Mrs. Taylor are eating dinner at the Steak House Restaurant. Suddenly Mr. Taylor begins choking. What should Mrs. Taylor do?

Jim and his brother are playing football. Jim tries to catch the ball, but falls down and breaks his finger. What should Jim's brother do?

Mrs. Wong's doctor tells her she has diabetes. What should she do to stay healthy?

Mr. Adams is cleaning his windows and falls off the ladder. He's unconscious. What should Mrs. Adams do?

Amy broke up with her boyfriend and now she's suffering from depression. What should she do to feel better?

Betsy and Paul are riding their mountain bikes. Paul falls off his bike and cuts his leg on a rock. There's a lot of blood. What should Betsy do?

Ms. Olsen has the flu and a high fever. What should she do?

George Mason's doctor tells him he has hypertension. George smokes, drinks, and eats a lot of red meat. What should he do?

Billy is only five years old. He has strep throat. What should his mother do to help him feel better?

Adam likes his job. One morning Adam falls and twists his ankle and it hurts a lot. What should Adam do?

I was at the doctor.
She examined my leg.
She told me to use a cane.

I was at the doctor.
She examined my leg.
She told me to use a walker.

I was at the doctor.
He measured my height and weight.
He told me to go on a diet.

I was at the doctor.
He measured my height and weight.
He told me to take vitamins.

I was at the doctor.
She cleaned and dressed a wound.
She told me to use lotion on my skin.

I was at the doctor.
She cleaned and dressed a wound.
She told me to use cream on my skin.

I was at the doctor.
He examined my eyes.
He told me I needed glasses.

I was at the doctor.
He examined my eyes.
He told me I needed surgery.

I was at the dentist.
He examined my teeth.
He told me I needed braces.

I was at the dentist.
He examined my teeth.
He told me I needed to see a specialist.

I was at the dentist.
She gave me Novocaine.
She told me to stop eating candy.

I was at the dentist.
She gave me Novocaine.
She told me to stop chewing gum.

I was at the dentist.
He drilled a cavity.
He told me to brush after every meal.

I was at the dentist.
He drilled a cavity.
He told me to brush before I go to bed.

I was at the dentist.
He filled a tooth.
He told me to stop eating cookies.

I was at the dentist.
He filled a tooth.
He told me to stop eating cake.

- Put your markers on *Start.*
- Take turns tossing the Game Cube (or flipping a coin) to move your marker around the board.
- Follow the instructions in each space.

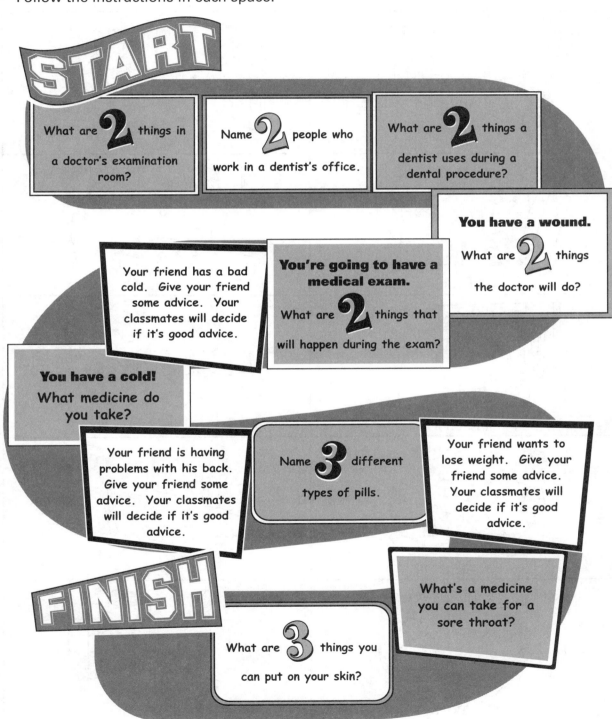

START

What are **2** things in a doctor's examination room?

Name **2** people who work in a dentist's office.

What are **2** things a dentist uses during a dental procedure?

You have a wound. What are **2** things the doctor will do?

Your friend has a bad cold. Give your friend some advice. Your classmates will decide if it's good advice.

You're going to have a medical exam. What are **2** things that will happen during the exam?

You have a cold! What medicine do you take?

Your friend is having problems with his back. Give your friend some advice. Your classmates will decide if it's good advice.

Name **3** different types of pills.

Your friend wants to lose weight. Give your friend some advice. Your classmates will decide if it's good advice.

FINISH

What's a medicine you can take for a sore throat?

What are **3** things you can put on your skin?

11.7 *Medical Treatment Board Game*
BOARD GAME
Word by Word Communication Games & Activity Masters, Page 65

- Spend 3 minutes looking very carefully at each of the following pictures.
- Put this Activity Master aside and complete Activity Master 107 to see how much information you can remember.

Boris

Morris

Christina

Angelina

Mr. Choi

Mr. Cho

Alan

Aaron

Mrs. Bright

Mrs. Wright

- Answer the questions below based on the illustrations on Activity Master 106.
- Look at Activity Master 106 again to check your answers. How much do you remember about these people?

1. Boris is seeing his (allergist   cardiologist) this morning.
   He's having (allergy   blood) tests.

2. Morris is seeing his (allergist   cardiologist) this morning.
   He's having (allergy   blood) tests.

3. Angelina is at the (doctor's office   hospital).
   She's talking to a (doctor   nurse).

4. Christina is at the (doctor's office   hospital).
   She's talking to a (doctor   nurse).

5. Mr. Cho is in the (radiology department   operating room).
   He's having (surgery   X-rays).

6. Mr. Choi is in the (radiology department   operating room).
   He's having (surgery   X-rays).

7. Alan is seeing his (physical therapist   audiologist).
   He's having (a hearing test   physical therapy).

8. Aaron is seeing his (physical therapist   audiologist).
   He's having (a hearing test   physical therapy).

9. Mrs. Wright is seeing her (counselor   acupuncturist) today.
   She's having (acupuncture   counseling).

10. Mrs. Bright is seeing her (counselor   acupuncturist) today.
    She's having (acupuncture   counseling).

Did You Brush Your Hair Today?   108

- Ask other students about personal hygiene and baby care.
- When you find someone who did the activity on your grid, have that person write his or her name in that square.
- The first student with the most signatures with the game.

Brush Your Hair? Name _____	Take a Bubble Bath? Name _____	Use a Shower Cap? Name _____
Use Dental Floss? Name _____	Use a Curling Iron? Name _____	Use a Blow Dryer? Name _____
Use Hairspray? Name _____	Use an Electric Razor? Name _____	Put on Mascara? Name _____
Change a Baby's Diaper? Name _____	Put on Cologne? Name _____	Give Formula to a Baby? Name _____
Polish Your Shoes? Name _____	Use Aftershave Lotion? Name _____	Use Hair Gel? Name _____

- Ask other students about their favorite subjects and extracurricular activities.
- When you find someone whose favorite subject or extracurricular activity is on your grid, have that person write his or her name in that square.
- The first student with the most signatures with the game.

Favorite Subject— English? Name _____	**Favorite Subject— History?** Name _____	**Favorite Subject— Biology?** Name _____
Favorite Subject— Music? Name _____	**Favorite Subject— Art?** Name _____	**Favorite Subject— P.E.?** Name _____
Play in the School Band? Name _____	**Play in the School Orchestra?** Name _____	**Sing in the School Chorus?** Name _____
Participate in Student Government? Name _____	**Write for the School Newspaper?** Name _____	**Work on the School Yearbook?** Name _____
Take Driver's Education? Name _____	**Like Physics?** Name _____	**Take Computer Science?** Name _____

- Put your markers on *Start*.
- Take turns tossing the Game Cube (or flipping a coin) to move your marker around the board.
- Follow the instructions in each space.

START

What are **2** types of schools for adults?

What are **2** types of schools for children?

What are **2** kinds of schools you can go to after college?

Put in order of age:
high school
nursery school
college
middle school
elementrary school

Name **5** different jobs for people who work in a school.

What are **2** "offices" in a school?

Name a science subject and a language subject.

What are **2** subjects that start with "g"?

What are **2** "music" extracurricular activities? SING YOUR ANSWER!

What are **2** "sports" extracurricular activities? Stand up and clap your hands as you answer!

What are your **3** favorite school subjects? SING YOUR ANSWER!

What are extracurricular activities where students "write things"? Write your answers on a piece of paper.

FINISH

12.2 *At School Board Game*
BOARD GAME
Word by Word Communication Games & Activity Masters, Page 69

ARITHMETIC	addition subtraction division
PARTS OF SPEECH	noun verb adjective
PLANETS	Jupiter Mars Saturn
SCIENCE EQUIPMENT	microscope test tube magnet
SOLID FIGURES	cube cylinder pyramid
TYPES OF SENTENCES	declarative interrogative exclamatory
ASTRONOMY	telescope observatory astronomer
TYPES OF LAND	forest meadow desert
TYPES OF LITERATURE	fiction non-fiction poetry
PUNCTUATION MARKS	period question mark comma

School Subject Concentration Cards

TYPES OF MATH	algebra calculus geometry
PLACES WITH WATER	river ocean bay
MEASUREMENTS	height weight depth
GEOMETRIC SHAPES	circle square rectangle
THE WRITING PROCESS	brainstorm organize revise
SCIENTIFIC METHOD	problem hypothesis procedure
SPACE EXPLORATION	satellite astronaut U.F.O.
TYPES OF LINES	straight parallel perpendicular
THE SOLAR SYSTEM	sun moon meteor
TYPES OF WRITING	letter postcard memo

School Subject Concentration Game
CONCENTRATION GAME
Word by Word Communication Games & Activity Masters, Page 71

© 2010 Pearson Education
Duplication for classroom use is permitted.

- Put your markers on *Start.*
- Take turns tossing the Game Cube (or flipping a coin) to move your marker around the board.
- Follow the instructions in each space.

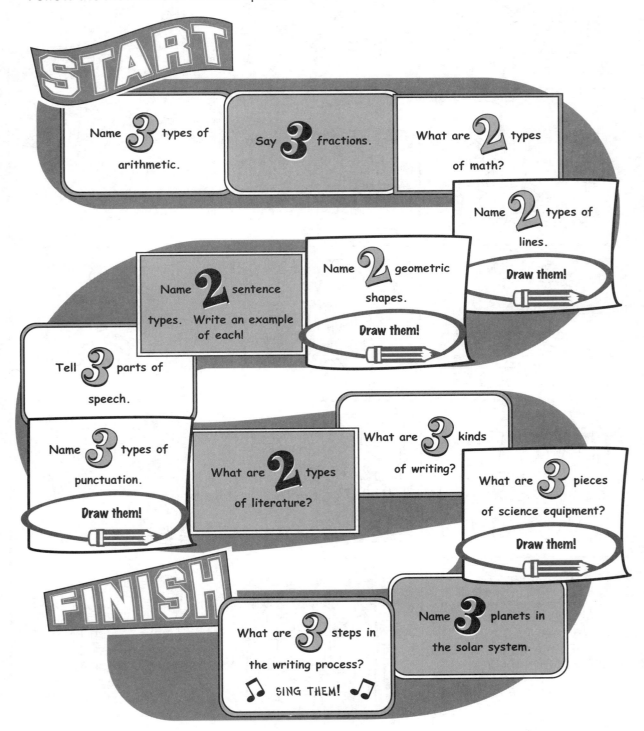

Occupation Cards

13.1 *What's My Occupation?*
LISTENING GRID
Word by Word Communication Games & Activity Masters, Page 73

© 2010 Pearson Education
Duplication for classroom use is permitted.

Occupation Word Clue Cards

Name That Job!
1. I like children.
2. I take care of children.
3. I come to children's homes when their parents go out.

BABYSITTER

Name That Job!
1. I work at weddings and other special occasions.
2. I take pictures.
3. I use a camera.

PHOTOGRAPHER

Name That Job!
1. I work in a restaurant.
2. I work with food.
3. I prepare food.

CHEF

Name That Job!
1. I work with animals.
2. I help them when they're sick.
3. People bring their animals to my office.

VETERINARIAN

Name That Job!
1. I work in an office.
2. I say hello to people when they come in.
3. I answer the telephone.

RECEPTIONIST

Name That Job!
1. I work in a hotel.
2. I vacuum and dust.
3. I clean.

HOUSEKEEPER

Name That Job!
1. I fix things.
2. I work in a repair shop.
3. I repair cars and trucks.

MECHANIC

Name That Job!
1. People listen to me.
2. I play in restaurants and clubs.
3. I play a musical instrument.

MUSICIAN

Name That Job!
1. I work outdoors.
2. I work with plants and trees.
3. I cut people's lawns.

GARDENER/LANDSCAPER

Name That Job!
1. I work in a restaurant.
2. I take people's orders.
3. I bring people their food.

WAITER/WAITRESS/SERVER

Name That Job!
1. I wear a uniform.
2. I work in an office building.
3. I protect people in the building.

SECURITY GUARD

Name That Job!
1. I can read and write in two languages.
2. I can speak two languages.
3. I help people understand each other.

TRANSLATOR

Name That Job!
1. I sit or stand in the front of the room.
2. I work with children and adults.
3. People learn things from me.

TEACHER

Name That Job!
1. I work in a doctor's office.
2. I meet with patients.
3. I help the doctor.

MEDICAL ASSISTANT/PHYSICIAN ASSISTANT

You need someone Monday through Friday.
The hours are 8:00 A.M. to 4:00 P.M.
You need someone who can use a computer.
You need a secretary.

You can work Monday through Friday.
You can work 8:00 A.M. to 4:00 P.M.
You can use a computer.
You want a job as a secretary.

You need someone Monday through Friday.
The hours are 8:00 A.M. to 4:00 P.M.
You need someone who can use a cash register.
You need a cashier.

You can work Monday through Friday.
You can work 8:00 A.M. to 4:00 P.M.
You can use a cash register.
You want a job as a cashier.

You need someone Monday through Friday.
The hours are 9:00 A.M. to 5:00 P.M.
You need someone who can speak Spanish.
You need a telemarketer.

You can work Monday through Friday.
You can work 9:00 A.M. to 5:00 P.M.
You can speak Spanish.
You want a job as a telemarketer.

You need someone Monday through Friday.
The hours are 9:00 A.M. to 5:00 P.M.
You need someone who can supervise people.
You need a supervisor.

You can work Monday through Friday.
You can work 9:00 A.M. to 5:00 P.M.
You can supervise people.
You want a job as a supervisor.

You need someone who can work evenings.
The hours are 6:00 P.M. to 11:00 P.M.
You need someone who can deliver pizzas.
You need a delivery person.

You can work evenings.
You can work 6:00 P.M. to 11:00 P.M.
You can deliver pizzas.
You want a job as a delivery person.

You need someone who can work evenings.
The hours are 6:00 P.M. to 11:00 P.M.
You need someone who can take inventory.
You need a stock clerk.

You can work evenings.
You can work 6:00 P.M. to 11:00 P.M.
You can take inventory.
You want a job as a stock clerk.

You need someone who can work evenings.
You need someone part-time.
You need someone who can use a computer.
You need a data entry clerk.

You can work evenings.
You can work part-time.
You can use a computer.
You want a job as a data entry clerk.

You need someone who can work evenings.
You need someone part-time.
You need someone who can use a computer.
You need a customer service representative.

You can work evenings.
You can work part-time.
You can use a computer.
You want a job as a customer service representative.

- Work with a group of students.
- These people are applying for a job as a receptionist in an international law office. They each have different skills and experience.
- Talk with students in your group about which person would be the *best one for the job*.
- Explain your reasons to the class.

Janet	Brian	Rose	David	Alice
available to work full-time	available to work part-time	available to work full-time	available to work full-time	available to work part-time
previous experience as a receptionist	previous experience as a translator	previous experience as a telemarketer	previous experience as a salesperson	previous experience as a customer service representative
often comes late to work	sometimes comes late to work	always comes to work on time	comes to work early	usually comes to work on time
takes the bus to work	walks to work	drives a car to work	takes the subway to work	takes the train to work
can speak only English	can speak English and Chinese	can speak English and Spanish	can speak only English	can speak English, Arabic, and Spanish
can use a computer	can use a computer	can't use a computer	can use a computer	can't use a computer

- You're an employee in a small office. Below is the list of tasks you were supposed to do today.
- Put a check next to the tasks you completed and leave the others blank.
- Your supervisor is going to ask you about the tasks—for example, "Did you sweep the coat closet yet?" If you put a check before that task, you respond, "Yes, I did. I swept the coat closet a little while ago." If you didn't put a check before that task, you respond, "No, I didn't. I'll sweep the coat closet in a little while."
- Compare checklists after you complete the activity.

To Do Today

____ sweep the coat closet

____ fix the coat rack

____ set up the conference room

____ rearrange the chairs in the conference room

____ dust the conference table

____ weigh letters on the postal scale

____ order a new paper shredder

____ put office supplies in the supply cabinet

____ rearrange the supply room

____ put mail in the employees' mailboxes

____ clean the storage room

____ fix the water cooler

____ sort the mail

____ repair the photocopier

Supervisor Checklist

- You're a supervisor in a small office. Below is the list of tasks your office assistant was supposed to do today.
- Ask if he or she completed each task—for example, "Did you sweep the coat closet?" If the employee completed that task, put a check before it on the list. If the employee didn't complete the task, leave the rule blank.
- After you have asked about all the tasks, compare checklists.

To Do Today

____ sweep the coat closet

____ fix the coat rack

____ set up the conference room

____ rearrange the chairs in the conference room

____ dust the conference table

____ weigh letters on the postal scale

____ order a new paper shredder

____ put office supplies in the supply cabinet

____ rearrange the supply room

____ put mail in the employees' mailboxes

____ clean the storage room

____ fix the water cooler

____ sort the mail

____ repair the photocopier

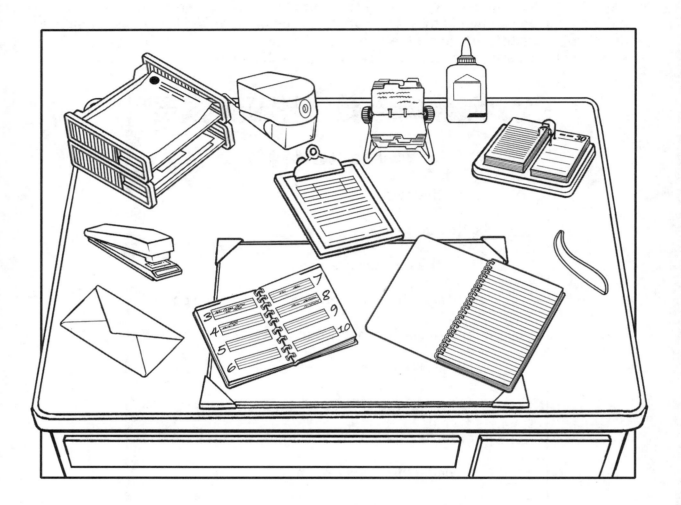

- There are 12 office supply items on the desk on Activity Master 120. How many can you remember?
- Look at Activity Master 120 again to check your answers.

Office Supplies on Diego's Desk

1. _____
2. _____
3. _____
4. _____
5. _____
6. _____
7. _____
8. _____
9. _____
10. _____
11. _____
12. _____

Workplace Board Game

- Put your markers on *Start*.
- Take turns tossing the Game Cube (or flipping a coin) to move your marker around the board.
- Follow the instructions in each space.

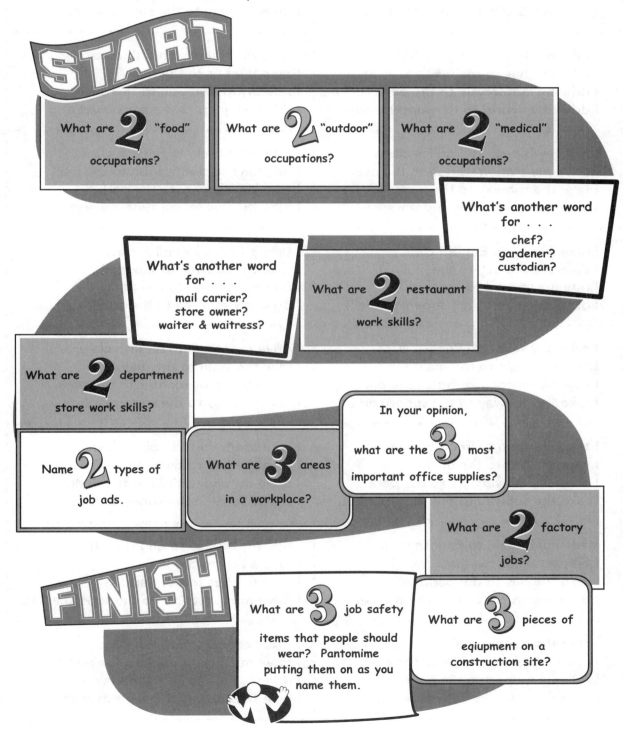

START

What are **2** "food" occupations?

What are **2** "outdoor" occupations?

What are **2** "medical" occupations?

What's another word for . . .
chef?
gardener?
custodian?

What's another word for . . .
mail carrier?
store owner?
waiter & waitress?

What are **2** restaurant work skills?

What are **2** department store work skills?

Name **2** types of job ads.

What are **3** areas in a workplace?

In your opinion, what are the **3** most important office supplies?

What are **2** factory jobs?

FINISH

What are **3** job safety items that people should wear? Pantomime putting them on as you name them.

What are **3** pieces of eqiupment on a construction site?

13.8 *Workplace Board Game*
BOARD GAME
Word by Word Communication Games & Activity Masters, Page 80

I take the bus to English class.
I take the train to the mall.
I ride my bicycle to the park.
I drive my S.U.V. to the supermarket.

I take the bus to English class.
I take the train to the mall.
I ride my bicycle to the park.
I drive my van to the supermarket.

I take the train to English class.
I take the bus to the mall.
I ride my motorcycle to the park.
I drive my hybrid to the supermarket.

I take the train to English class.
I take the bus to the mall.
I ride my motorcycle to the park.
I drive my jeep to the supermarket.

I ride my bicycle to English class.
I drive my station wagon to the mall.
I take the subway to the park.
I take the train to the supermarket.

I ride my bicycle to English class.
I drive my station wagon to the mall.
I take the subway to the park.
I take the bus to the supermarket.

I take a ferry to English class.
I take the subway to the mall.
I ride my moped to the park.
I drive my jeep to the supermarket.

I take a ferry to English class.
I take the subway to the mall.
I ride my moped to the park.
I drive my minivan to the supermarket.

I drive my sedan to English class.
I take the train to the mall.
I ride my motor scooter to the park.
I take the subway to the supermarket.

I drive my sedan to English class.
I take the train to the mall.
I ride my motor scooter to the park.
I take the bus to the supermarket.

I take the train to English class.
I take the bus to the mall.
I drive my convertible to the park.
I take the subway to the supermarket.

I take the train to English class.
I take the bus to the mall.
I drive my convertible to the park.
I take a ferry to the supermarket.

I ride my bicycle to English class.
I take a taxi to the mall.
I take the bus to the park.
I drive my truck to the supermarket.

I ride my bicycle to English class.
I take a taxi to the mall.
I take the bus to the park.
I drive my sports car to the supermarket.

I take the bus to English class.
I drive my pickup truck to the mall.
I ride my moped to the park.
I take the train the supermarket.

I take the bus to English class.
I drive my pickup truck to the mall.
I ride my moped to the park.
I take the subway the supermarket.

14.1 *Transportation Match Game*
MATCHING GAME
Word by Word Communication Games & Activity Masters, Page 81

14.2 *What's the Car Part?*
LISTENING GRID
Word by Word Communication Games & Activity Masters, Page 82

Transportation Board Game

- Put your markers on *Start.*
- Take turns tossing the Game Cube (or flipping a coin) to move your marker around the board.
- Follow the instructions in each space.

START

What are **3** types of public transportation?

Name **3** parts of a train station.

Name **3** parts of a subway station.

What are **3** things associated with a bus?

Pick a Traffic Sign Card!
___
Explain what the sign means.

Draw a picture of a vehicle.
Everyone has to guess what kind of vehicle it is.

What are **3** types of vehicles for a family?

What are the **4** compass directions?

What are **3** road test instructions?

Name **2** parts on the front of a car and **2** parts on the back of a car.

Pick a Traffic Sign Card!
___
Explain what the sign means.

FINISH

Name **3** things on the driver's side of the car.

Name **2** things on an instrument panel of a car.

Name **2** things under the hood of a car.

- Work with a partner. Look at these highways.
- There are seven differences between Interstate 70 and Interstate 99.
- Talk with your partner about the differences and write them in the chart below.

On Interstate 70	**On Interstate 99**
1. A car is going over a bridge.	**1.** A truck is going over a bridge.
2.	**2.**
3.	**3.**
4.	**4.**
5.	**5.**
6.	**6.**
7.	**7.**

- Work with a partner. Look at these highways.
- There are seven differences between Interstate 70 and Interstate 99.
- Talk with your partner about the differences and write them in the chart below.

On Interstate 70	**On Interstate 99**
1. *A car is going over a bridge.*	**1.** *A truck is going over a bridge.*
2.	**2.**
3.	**3.**
4.	**4.**
5.	**5.**
6.	**6.**
7.	**7.**

14.4 *What's Different About These Highways?*
PICTURE DIFFERENCES
Word by Word Communication Games & Activity Masters, Page 84

- Put your markers on *Start.*
- Take turns tossing the Game Cube (or flipping a coin) to move your marker around the board.
- Follow the instructions in each space.

START

What are **3** areas in an airport?

Name **3** people who work at the airport.

What are **3** things you do at airport security?

Name **3** things associated with "baggage."

Pantomime an air travel action. Everyone has to guess what you're doing.

What are **2** things you do when you board a plane?

What are **3** safety items on an airplane?

Name **2** people who work on an airplane.

You're an airplane pilot!

Make an announcement to your passengers!

Name **3** people who work in a hotel.

What are **3** different areas inside a hotel?

FINISH

You're a desk clerk in a hotel. Greet a new guest and tell the guest about the hotel.

14.5 *Airplane & Hotel Board Game*
BOARD GAME
Word by Word Communication Games & Activity Masters, Page 85

14.6 *Roberto Took a Trip*
TELL-A-STORY
Word by Word Communication Games & Activity Masters, Page 86

- Ask other students about their favorite hobbies, crafts, and games.
- When you find someone whose favorite hobby, craft, or game is on your grid, have that person write his or her name in that square.
- The first student with the most signatures with the game.

Sew? Name _____	**Draw?** Name _____	**Do Origami?** Name _____
Make Pottery? Name _____	**Paint?** Name _____	**Collect Stamps?** Name _____
Build Models? Name _____	**Play Cards?** Name _____	**Browse the Web?** Name _____
Play Board Games? Name _____	**Go to Museums?** Name _____	**Go to Concerts?** Name _____
Go to Craft Fairs? Name _____	**Go to the Mountains?** Name _____	**Go to the Zoo?** Name _____

- Work with a partner. Look at these beaches.
- There are eight differences between the two beaches.
- Talk with your partner about the differences and write them in the chart below.

At the Surfside Beach	At the Bayside Beach
1. A boy is flying a kite.	**1.** A girl is flying a kite.
2.	**2.**
3.	**3.**
4.	**4.**
5.	**5.**
6.	**6.**
7.	**7.**
8.	**8.**

15.3 *What's Different About These Beaches?*
PICTURE DIFFERENCES
Word by Word Communication Games & Activity Masters, Page 89

- Work with a partner. Look at these beaches.
- There are eight differences between the two beaches.
- Talk with your partner about the differences and write them in the chart below.

At the Surfside Beach	At the Bayside Beach
1. A boy is flying a kite.	**1.** A girl is flying a kite.
2.	**2.**
3.	**3.**
4.	**4.**
5.	**5.**
6.	**6.**
7.	**7.**
8.	**8.**

15.3 *What's Different About These Beaches?*
PICTURE DIFFERENCES
Word by Word Communication Games & Activity Masters, Page 89

- Put your markers on *Start*.
- Take turns tossing the Game Cube (or flipping a coin) to move your marker around the board.
- Follow the instructions in each space.

START

Where are **3** places to go for recreation?

What are **3** things you see at the park?

Name **3** things in a playground.

Name **3** things you take with you to the beach.

Name **3** individual sports.

What are **3** things you take with you when you go camping?

What are **3** types of outdoor recreation? Pantomime each one as you name it!

What are **3** things you take with you when you go hiking?

What are **3** things you take with you when you go on a picnic?

Name **2** pieces of workout equipment.

You're going to have a very busy weekend! Sing a song about **3** things you're going to do for recreation.

FINISH

You're on TV!

Present a one-minute commercial for a new sports club.

Tell all the activities that are available!

Think of an individual sport.

DESCRIBE IT!

Everyone has to guess what it is.

15.4 *Recreation Board Game*
BOARD GAME
Word by Word Communication Games & Activity Masters, Page 90

You need a bow and arrow and a target for this activity. _____	You need a racket and birdie for this activity. _____	You need goggles and a racket for this activity. _____
You need a flying disc for this activity. _____	You need gloves and trunks for this activity. _____	You need a saddle, reins, and stirrups for this activity. _____
You need a uniform and mat for this activity. _____	You need a sleeping bag, tent, and lantern for this activity. _____	You need a compass and trail map for this activity. _____
You need a harness and rope for this activity. _____	You need a blanket and thermos for this activity. _____	You need barbells and weights for this activity. _____

Sports & Exercise Action Board Game   138

- Put your markers on *Start.*
- Take turns tossing the Game Cube (or flipping a coin) to move your marker around the board.
- Follow the instructions in each space.

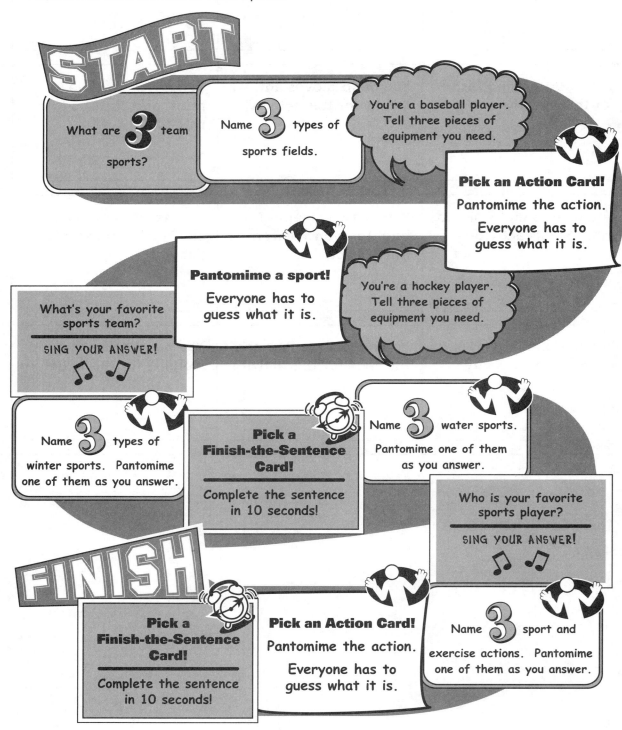

15.6 *Sport & Exercise Action Board Game*
BOARD GAME
Word by Word Communication Games & Activity Masters, Page 92

© 2010 Pearson Education
Duplication for classroom use is permitted.

bend	bounce	catch	deep knee bend
dive	dribble	hit	hop
jump	jumping jack	kick	lift
pitch	push-up	reach	run
shoot	sit-up	skip	stretch
swim	swing	throw	walk

You use bindings and poles when you go . . .

You use a saucer when you go . . .

You use paddles when you go . . .

You wear a bathing suit when you go . . .

You use a mask and fins when you go . . .

You use a wet suit and tank when you go . . .

You use a reel, net, and bait when you go . . .

You use a bat, ball, and glove when you play . . .

You use a stick and puck when you play . . .

You use a backboard and hoop when you play . . .

You play on a rink when you play . . .

You play on a court when you play . . .

You use a helmet and shoulder pads when you play . . .

You wear shinguards when you play . . .

You need a bow and arrow and a target. What's the sport?	You play this on a table with a paddle and net. What's the sport?	You play this on a table with a stick and balls. What's the sport?
This sport uses a ball and you have to wear special shoes. What's the sport?	You sit on a saddle and hold reins. What's the sport?	You play this on a court with five players on each team. What's the sport?
You play this on a court or in the sand. What's the sport?	The catcher has a mitt and wears a mask. What's the sport?	You play this on a court with five players on each team. What's the sport?
You can only do this in the winter on frozen ice. What's the sport?	You use oars when you do this. What's the sport?	You use a mask and fins when you do this. What's the sport?
You use a sailboard when you do this. What's the sport?	You use a rod and bait when you do this. What's the sport?	

You use a racquet and safety goggles when you play this. What's the sport?	You use clubs and a special ball when you play this. What's the sport?	You use barbells and weights when you do this. What's the sport?
You wear trunks and special gloves when you do this. What's the sport?	Players wear a helmet and shoulder pads when you play this. What's the sport?	Players use a puck and stick when you play this. What's the sport?
Players wear shinguards to play this. What's the sport?	You use a face guard and stick when you play this. What's the sport?	You have blades and guards when you do this. What's the sport?
You use a dish or saucer when you do this. What's the sport?	You wear a special suit and cap when you do this. What's the sport?	You need an air tank and mask when you do this. What's the sport?
You use special skis and a towrope when you do this. What's the sport?	You use a small boat and oars when you do this. What's the sport?	

What Are Your Favorite Types of Entertainment? **143**

- Ask other students about their favorite types of music, plays, movies, and TV programs.
- When you find someone whose favorite is on your grid, have that person write his or her name in that square.
- The first student with the most signatures with the game.

Classical Music? Name _____	**Rock Music?** Name _____	**Reggae Music?** Name _____
Tragedies? Name _____	**Musical Comedies?** Name _____	**Mystery Movies?** Name _____
Foreign Films? Name _____	**Documentary Movies?** Name _____	**Horror Movies?** Name _____
Action Movies? Name _____	**TV News Programs?** Name _____	**TV Reality Shows?** Name _____
TV Sitcoms? Name _____	**TV Shopping Programs?** Name _____	**TV Talk Shows?** Name _____

- Put your markers on *Start.*
- Take turns tossing the Game Cube (or flipping a coin) to move your marker around the board.
- Follow the instructions in each space.

- Work with a partner. Look at these zoos.
- There are nine differences between the East Coast Zoo and the West Coast Zoo.
- Talk with your partner about the differences and write them in the chart below.

EAST COAST ZOO

The East Coast Zoo has . . .	The West Coast Zoo has . . .
1. a camel	**1.** a llama
2.	**2.**
3.	**3.**
4.	**4.**
5.	**5.**
6.	**6.**
7.	**7.**
8.	**8.**
9.	**9.**

- Work with a partner. Look at these zoos.
- There are nine differences between the East Coast Zoo and the West Coast Zoo.
- Talk with your partner about the differences and write them in the chart below.

The East Coast Zoo has . . .	The West Coast Zoo has . . .
1. a camel	**1.** a llama
2.	**2.**
3.	**3.**
4.	**4.**
5.	**5.**
6.	**6.**
7.	**7.**
8.	**8.**
9.	**9.**

16.1 *What's Different About These Zoos?*
PICTURE DIFFERENCES
Word by Word Communication Games & Activity Masters, Page 96

	Mosquitoes usually live for about two weeks.		Peacocks can live twenty years.
	Turtles can live over 100 years.		Whales can weigh 30 tons.
	Alligators have between 74 and 80 teeth.		Grasshoppers can "sing."
	Hummingbirds love the color red.		Ostriches can't fly.
	Otters swim on their backs.		Owls can turn their heads 270 degrees.
	Parrots can learn to talk.		Dolphins are the most intelligent mammals.
	Jellyfish kill more people than any other marine animal.		Scorpions live in the desert.
	Eagles are the national symbol of the United States.		Robins' eggs are blue.

- Answer the questions below based on the information on Activity Master 147.
- Look at Activity Master 147 again to check your answers. How many interesting animal facts did you remember?

alligator	hummingbird	otter	robin
dolphin	jellyfish	owl	scorpion
eagle	mosquito	parrot	turtle
grasshopper	ostrich	peacock	whale

1. Which bird can't fly? _____

2. Which insect usually lives for about two weeks? _____

3. Which sea animal is the most intelligent mammal? _____

4. Which amphibian can weigh 30 tons? _____

5. Which bird can learn to talk? _____

6. Which sea animal kills the most people? _____

7. Which insect lives in the desert? _____

8. Which amphibian can live over 100 years? _____

9. While bird can turn its head 270 degrees? _____

10. Which sea animal swims on its back? _____

11. Which bird can live twenty years? _____

12. Which amphibian has between 74 and 80 teeth? _____

13. Which bird loves the color red? _____

14. Which bird has blue eggs? _____

15. Which insect can "sing"? _____

16. Which bird is the national symbol of the United States? _____

Name two insects that begin with the letter "b."	Name three different fish.	Name three sea animals.	Finish the sentence: My favorite fish is the . . .
What are three animals that have fur?	Which animal has hooves?	Name three animals that live in North America.	Name three animals that live in Asia.
Which animal has quills?	What's another word for "buffalo"?	Name an animal with whiskers.	What's another word for "ray"?
Name three animals that live in Africa.	Which animal has a hump?	Which animal has a mane?	Which animal has a pouch?
What are three insects that fly?	Complete the sentence: A bee lives in a ____.	Name three sea animals.	Finish the sentence: My favorite animal is the . . . because . . .
Finish the sentence: My favorite sea animal is the . . . because . . .			

16.3 *Name That Animal!*
TEAM COMPETITION
Word by Word Communication Games & Activity Masters, Page 98

Name three animals that begin with the letter "g."	Name two amphibians and one reptile.	Finish the sentence. My "least" favorite insect is the . . .	What are three animals that have tails?
Name an animal that has antlers.	What are two kinds of bears?	Name three animals that live in South America.	Name three animals that live in Australia.
What's another word for "possum"?	Name an animal with spots.	What's another word for "firefly"?	What are four common household pets?
Which animal has horns?	Which animal has a tusk?	Which animal has stripes?	Which sea animal has a tusk?
Name two birds that begin with the letter "p."	What insect does a caterpillar become?	What are two amphibians with tails?	Finish the sentence: My favorite bird is the . . . because . . .
Think of an animal. Make the sound that animal makes. Everyone has to guess the animal.			

16.3 *Name That Animal!*
TEAM COMPETITION
Word by Word Communication Games & Activity Masters, Page 98

- Work with a partner. (Don't show this chart to your partner.)
- There are several weather disasters taking place in many parts of the world today. Ask your partner questions about what's happening in different places.
- Write the answers in the chart below.
- Compare events with your partner.

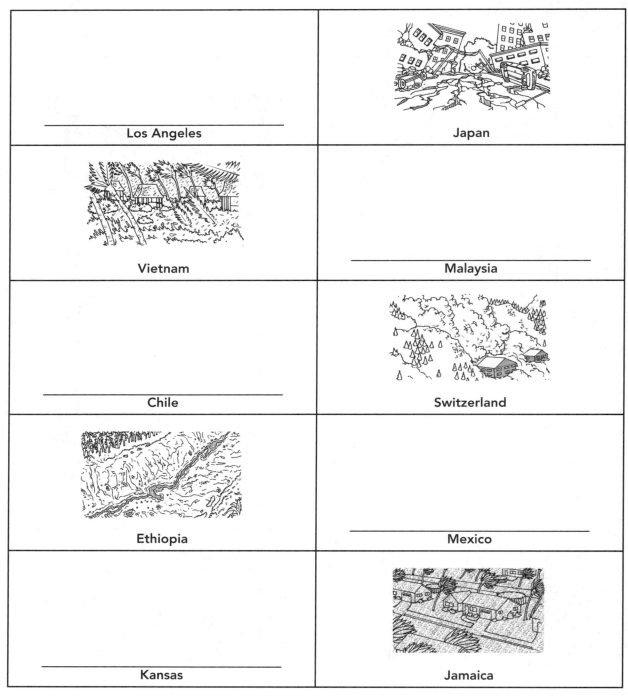

_____ Los Angeles	Japan
Vietnam	_____ Malaysia
_____ Chile	Switzerland
Ethiopia	_____ Mexico
_____ Kansas	Jamaica

- Work with a partner. (Don't show this chart to your partner.)
- There are several weather disasters taking place in many parts of the world today. Ask your partner questions about what's happening in different places.
- Write the answers in the chart below.
- Compare events with your partner.

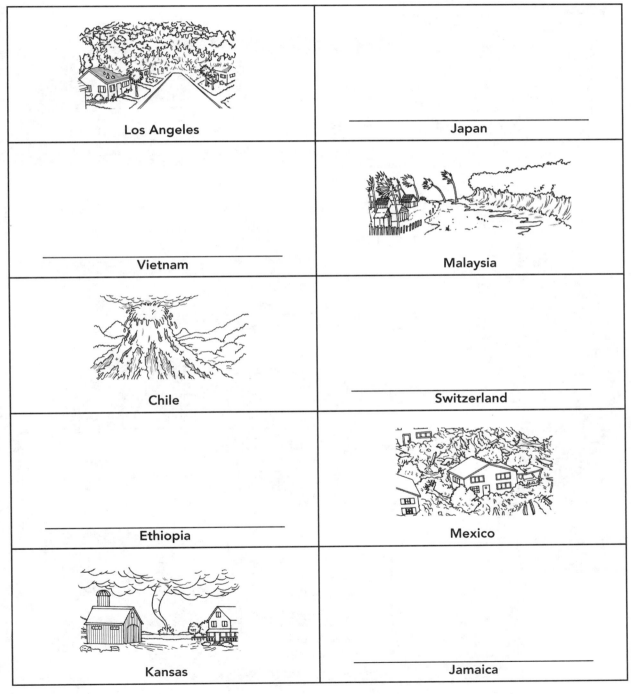

Los Angeles	_____ Japan
_____ Vietnam	Malaysia
Chile	_____ Switzerland
_____ Ethiopia	Mexico
Kansas	_____ Jamaica

Environment & Nature Board Game

154

- Put your markers on *Start.*
- Take turns tossing the Game Cube (or flipping a coin) to move your marker around the board.
- Follow the instructions in each space.

START

What are **3** sources of energy?

Tell **3** ways to conserve energy.

What are **3** environmental problems?

Name **3** natural disasters.

What are **3** parts of a tree? **Draw them!**

Tell the names of **3** trees.

Tell the names of **3** flowers.

What are **2** poisonous plants?

What are **3** flowers that are yellow?

What are **2** flowers that are white?

FINISH

Draw a flower. Everyone has to guess what flower it is.

What are **2** flowers that are red?

16.6 *Environment & Nature Board Game*
BOARD GAME
Word by Word Communication Games & Activity Masters, Page 101

© 2010 Pearson Education
Duplication for classroom use is permitted.

U.S. Government Board Game

156

- Put your markers on *Start.*
- Take turns tossing the Game Cube (or flipping a coin) to move your marker around the board.
- Follow the instructions in each space.

START

What branch of government makes the laws?

What's the name of the building where the senators work?

Complete the sentence:
The Supreme Court justices work in the _____ branch.

What branch of government enforces the laws?

Complete the sentence:
The representatives work in the _____ branch.

What's the name of the building where the vice-president works?

Who works in the legislative branch?

Complete the sentence:
The president works in the _____ branch.

What branch of government explains the laws?

What's the name of the building where the Supreme Court justices work?

Who works in the judicial branch?

FINISH

You're the president!
Give a short speech to the classmates in your group. Tell about your job.

Who works in the executive branch?

17.2A   *U.S. Government Board Game*
BOARD GAME
Word by Word Communication Games & Activity Masters, Page 103

Which amendment guarantees freedom of speech?	Which amendment guarantees freedom of religion?	Which amendment established income taxes?	Which amendment gave African-Americans the right to vote?
Which amendment gave citizens eighteen years and older the right to vote?	Which war began in 1775?	When did the colonists declare their independence?	What was added to the Constitution in 1791?
When did the Civil War begin?	Who signed the Emancipation Proclamation?	Who invented the light bulb?	When did World War I end?
When did the Great Depression begin?	When did the Korean War end?	Who was the first man on the moon?	When did the Vietnam War end?
In which month is Martin Luther King, Jr. Day?	In which month is Memorial Day?	What holiday is on October 31st?	When is Veterans Day?

17.3A *U.S. Civics Question Game*
TEAM COMPETITION
Word by Word Communication Games & Activity Masters, Page 104

Which amendment ended slavery?

Which amendment gave women the right to vote?

Which amendment guarantees freedom of the press?

Which amendment guarantees freedom of assembly?

What are the first ten amendments to the Constitution called?

When did the Revolutionary War end?

Who was the first president of the United States?

When did the Civil War end?

What did Alexander Graham Bell invent?

When did World War I begin?

When did women get the right to vote?

When did World War II begin?

When did the Korean War begin?

What famous event took place in 1963?

When did the Vietnam War begin?

When did terrorists attack the United States?

When is Valentine's Day?

When is Independence Day?

In which month is Thanksgiving?

When is Christmas?

- Put your markers on *Start.*
- Take turns tossing the Game Cube (or flipping a coin) to move your marker around the board.
- Follow the instructions in each space.

START

Tell **3** forms of identification you have.

Name the **3** branches of the U.S. government.

Who works in the Capitol Building?

What document begins with the words, "We the People"?

How many "freedoms" does the 1st Amendment guarantee? What are they?

What are the first 10 amendments to the Constitution called?

Name **3** wars in American history.

Who were **2** important inventors? What did they invent?

In 25 seconds . . .
Name **3** U.S. holidays and give their dates.

What is a police officer required to read to a suspect in a crime?

FINISH

Name **3** different steps in the path to citizenship.

Name **3** citizens' rights and responsibilities.

- Ask other students about their travel experiences.
- When you find someone who did the activity on your grid, have that person write his or her name in that square.
- The first student with the most signatures with the game.

Go on a Cruise? **(Where did you go?)** Name _____	**Go on a Bus Tour?** **(Where did you go?)** Name _____	**Take a Long** **Train Trip?** **(Where did you go?)** Name _____
Go on a Business Trip? **(Where did you go?)** Name _____	**Go on a Boat Trip?** **(Where did you go?)** Name _____	**Go on a Ski Trip?** **(Where did you go?)** Name _____
Go on a Study Tour? **(Where did you go?)** Name _____	**Go on a Safari?** **(Where did you go?)** Name _____	**Book a Trip Online?** **(Where did you go?)** Name _____
Book a Trip at a **Travel Agency?** **(Where did you go?)** Name _____	**Get a Visa from** **Another Country** **(Which Country?)** Name _____	**Stay in a Suite** **at a Hotel?** **(Which hotel?)** Name _____
Get Room Service **at a Hotel?** **(Which hotel?** **What did you order?)** Name _____	**Lose Your Passport?** **(What happened?)** Name _____	**Lose Your Baggage** **Claim Check?** **(What happened?)** Name _____

International Travel Board Game

163

- Put your markers on *Start.*
- Take turns tossing the Game Cube (or flipping a coin) to move your marker around the board.
- Follow the instructions in each space.

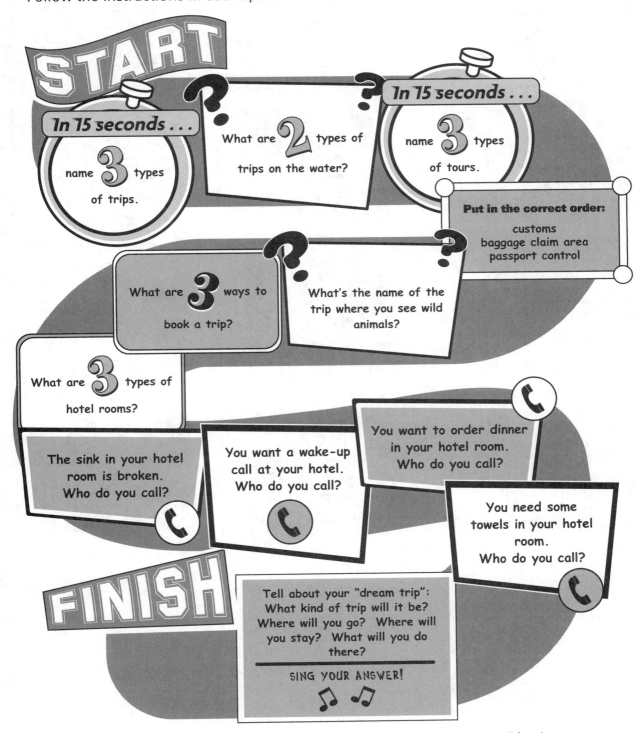

START

In 15 seconds . . . name **3** types of trips.

What are **2** types of trips on the water?

In 15 seconds . . . name **3** types of tours.

Put in the correct order:
customs
baggage claim area
passport control

What are **3** ways to book a trip?

What's the name of the trip where you see wild animals?

What are **3** types of hotel rooms?

The sink in your hotel room is broken. Who do you call?

You want a wake-up call at your hotel. Who do you call?

You want to order dinner in your hotel room. Who do you call?

You need some towels in your hotel room. Who do you call?

FINISH

Tell about your "dream trip": What kind of trip will it be? Where will you go? Where will you stay? What will you do there?

SING YOUR ANSWER!

17.2B   *International Travel Board Game*
BOARD GAME
Word by Word Communication Games & Activity Masters, Page 109

- Work with a partner. (Don't show this diagram to your partner.) You also each have a set of *Tourist Activity Cards*.
- Partner A chooses two or more *Tourist Activity Cards* and places them on each day of the week.
- Partner B asks Yes/No questions in order to find out what Partner A did on each day of the trip, then arranges the cards on his or her diagram based on the answers.
- Compare with your partner's diagram to see if your cards are in the same days of the week.
- Then switch roles. Partner B chooses the cards and Partner A asks the questions.

My Trip to _____

Monday	Tuesday
Wednesday	**Thursday**

17.4B *My Trip*

17.5B *Sofia's Vacation*
TELL-A-STORY
Word by Word Communication Games & Activity Masters, Page 112

Tourist Board Game

- Put your markers on *Start.*
- Take turns tossing the Game Cube (or flipping a coin) to move your marker around the board.
- Follow the instructions in each space.

START

What are **2** types of tours?

Name **3** places where tourists often go.

What's your favorite souvenir? Where did you get it?

You're a tourist in a new city. You want to go to a nice restaurant. You also want to have a car. What do you have to do?

Complete **3** common tourist requests: "May I _____?"

What are your **3** favorite tourist activities?
_____
SING YOUR ANSWER! ♪ ♫

Ask permission to do something in a museum. Have a classmate respond.

Ask permission to do something in a store. Have a classmate respond.

You're a tourist in a new city. You meet someone who lives there. What are **3** common questions a local person might ask you?

A police officer sees someone and wants that person to stop. What are **3** things the police officer can say?

You're a tourist, and you're in trouble! What should you shout?

FINISH

When someone speaks *very quickly,* what are **3** things you can say? Role play conversations with three *fast-talking* classmates.

You want to know how to say a word in English. What do you ask?

Game Index

Notes

Notes

Notes

Notes

Notes

Notes

Notes

Notes

Notes

Notes